AMBUSH
The Story of Bill Keys

AMBUSH

The Story
of Bill Keys

By
Art Kidwell

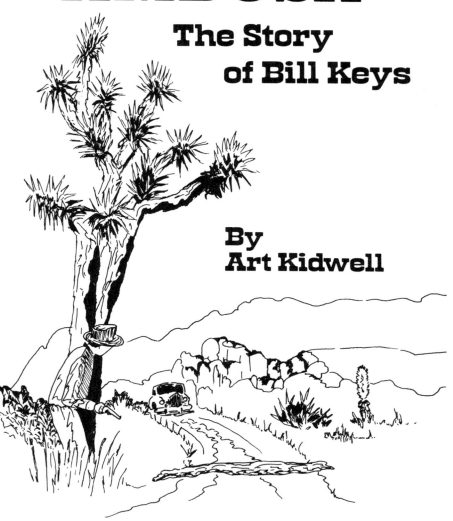

DESERT MOON PRESS
Twentynine Palms, CA

First Printing 1979 Pioneer Press
Second Printing 1995 Desert Moon Press

DESERT MOON PRESS
Twentynine Palms, CA 92277

Library of Congress Catalog Card No. 79-90977
ISBN 0-914330-31-4 cloth
ISBN 0-9617961-5-4 paper

"Truth will ultimately prevail when there are pains taken to bring it to light."

George Washington

Acknowledgement

Thirty-six years ago two men met on an isolated dirt road in California's Mojave Desert. The two were neighbors, and both were as tough as the environment in which they lived. One planned an ambush for the other on that May morning in 1943. When the gunfire stopped, one of the two lay dead in what was probably one of the last gunfights in the West.

Riverside, San Bernardino, and Los Angeles newspapers gave considerable coverage to the shooting, as well as to the trial of its survivor, William F. Keys. By this time, he was already a desert legend and was no stranger to conflict, controversy, or to newspapermen. For Bill Keys was part of an era that has long passed. He was one of the last of a dying breed—a true man of the Old West. The mere mention of his name brings back visions of a time in the desert when gold miners searched its mountains, cowboys roamed its valleys, and feuds between men were settled with gunfire.

Much has been written about Bill and his equally remarkable wife, Frances. Newspaper and magazine articles concentrate on his conflicts, his mines, and his ranch. Today, ten years after his death, countless tales still circulate about a man that, other than his family and closest friends, few people really knew. For his quick wit, dedication to hard work, generosity to others, artistic ability, and love of nature are not the ingredients that make legends.

My goal in telling Bill's story is to clear up some of the myth that surrounds his greatest conflict, his infamous

vii

gunfight with Worth Bagley, as well as to share some of the life history of this desert pioneer for those who may not be familiar with the history of our area. This project was aided by a number of individuals who have all contributed to the finished work.

Janaan Dawson and Ed Commerly of the Clerk's Office, Riverside County Court, and Chief Clerk Robert Ford, Mary Sather and Bernice Kaz of the State Court of Appeals, San Bernardino were most helpful in locating the three huge volumes of court transcripts of the Keys trial from State Archives.

Ken Peterson of Wiefels and Son Mortuary, Banning, provided information concerning Worth Bagley's funeral arrangements, while the staff at the Los Angeles National Cemetery helped to locate his grave.

Vivian Fowler at Joshua Tree National Monument located letters, weather information, and file material concerning the history of the Monument during the past thirty years. My three years on the Monument's staff afforded me the opportunity for an in-depth study of the Keys Ranch artifacts, while numerous visitors on my Keys Ranch tours willingly shared memories of much earlier trips there. From these bits and pieces emerged a more complete understanding of the Keys family's ranch life.

Many other friends of the Keys family contributed valuable information and stories. The most notable were: Oran Booth, Ada Hatch, Evelyn Hutchinson, Daisy Kiler, Frank Kiler, Gladys Lindsay, Bob Michaels, Paulo Krucero, Katherine Randolph, Ed Scoggins, Bill Wessel, Jo and Jim Wakefield, and the late Grace Brock. Grace was a constant source of stories and encouragement, as was Ada Hatch who went out of her way to locate early photographs, as well as to provide intimate glimpses of early homesteading days in Twentynine Palms. Barry Feinstein designed the dust jacket and gave me a taped interview that he had done with Bill Keys a year before his death. Cheryl Erickson, Twentynine Palms librarian, provided names, photographs, and transcripts concerning the early history of our area from the fine Local Historical Collection assembled under her capable supervision. Leah Foerster and Erni Escalante helped with editing, while Alyn Helms typed the final manuscript and Alice Siebecker did the title page drawing. To all of these individuals I would like to express my deep appreciation for their valuable contributions.

Special thanks must be reserved for Willis and Gwyn Keys, who believed in the project from its start and were a continual source of encouragement. In the three years that we have been friends, they have willingly shared their time, private memories, and family photographs. They never refused to answer my endless questions and made me welcome in their home, treating me as a member of their family. Without their assistance, this book could never have been written. The result is hopefully a reflection of their trust, confidence, and profound friendship, and in grateful appreciation, I dedicate this book to them.

Art Kidwell

September 1979
Twentynine Palms, California

Introduction

April 1940

The frail-looking woman had been busy all morning sweeping and cleaning. Because of frequent desert winds, she had quickly realized the sheer impossibility of keeping sand and dust out of the concrete block and adobe-walled house that she now called home. A never ending task, yet it was one of her daily chores.

At noon she stopped to check on the meal that was simmering on the kitchen stove. Isabelle hoped that her husband would be pleased with the stew she had prepared with the jackrabbit he had shot early that morning in the wash behind the house. He was an excellent shot, and here in this remote area, he never ventured anywhere without his holster and pistol.

Leaning out the kitchen door, she called her husband's name. Receiving no answer, she moved the stew pot to the back of the wood-burning stove and set out in search of him. As she walked east toward their well, her steps fell into a steady rhythmic pattern on the dirt road that wound its way through Joshua trees and yuccas. Along both sides of the roadway, as far as she could see, were spring wildflowers. A yellow carpet of dandelions, Coreopsis, Eriophyllum, Keysia, and brittlebush covered the desert floor. She felt the warming rays of the sun on her face, and her thoughts turned back to that time, three years ago, when she had decided to move to her sister's in Yucca Valley. The desert climate had been good for her, and her strength and health had slowly improved.

Then, only four months ago, her life had changed once again. She had met and married a man who had lived here in the desert off and on since 1936. Theirs had been a quick courtship, and she was only now beginning to realize how little she really knew about him. As time passed, she discovered that her husband had strange moods and at times, a violent temper. She was lonely at their isolated ranch. The nearest neighbor was some three miles away, and she wished again, as she had many times these past few months, for a friend or neighbor not quite so distant. However, her husband did not share this desire and seemed perfectly content with this isolation. She had quickly learned to say nothing to offend or upset him. For at these times, she was actually concerned about her own safety.

Her ten-minute walk ended a half mile away at their well. The tank truck which hauled water to the cistern adjacent to the house was parked nearby, but no one was in sight. She looked around, then crossed through the fence at the cattle-guard and headed up the dirt road to a place where she had previously found her husband. Two hundred yards away she found him crouched down in the dry wash that partially ran parallel with the road.

"Worth, your lunch is ready," she called as she approached him.

Her forty-year-old husband looked up suddenly, got to his feet and walked toward her. She could see that his pistol was in his hand.

"Worth, lunch is ready. I called but when you didn't answer, I decided to come looking for you before everything got cold."

It seemed the man did not hear a word she said. His mind was on something more important as he muttered, "One of these days, I'll get rid of that 'old goat.' If I ever catch him alone out here and without witnesses . . . "

His wife made no comment on this pronouncement but turned to head back the way she had come. He put the gun back into its holster and with a few quick steps caught up with her. Then Isabelle and Worth Bagley continued along the dirt road that led to their house and disappeared inside.

The
Shooting

I

May 11, 1943
Tuesday

With a firm pull, he stretched the canvas belt from his pump and slipped it over the wheel hub of the old Fairbanks-Morse engine. He then grasped the flywheel, and with a powerful throw, he spun the machine into life. The one-cylinder engine chugged slowly, almost irregularly, until it reached full throttle. As it smoothed out into a regular pattern, the sound of cool water coming from the depths of the well echoed up through the pipes and began to splash into the cattle trough nearby. Then with a satisfaction that comes from accomplishing even little things well, he stepped back from the engine, wiped the sweat from his brow, and continued his early morning chores.

Like the old engine that he was constantly repairing, Bill Keys didn't look anywhere near his age. The medium-sized man was in fine physical condition. His face and hands were deeply tanned. His muscles were taut, having been tempered by many years of hard work under the California desert sun. When he removed the hat which he always wore while working outside, one noticed the fringe of black hair on the sides was sprinkled with grey.

Although he would be sixty-four years old in September, he was still busy with one project or another. After moving here to the southern part of the Mojave Desert a little more than thirty-three years ago, he had learned the necessity of developing several skills in order to survive in the then isolated area. Today he was an accomplished stonemason, carpenter, blacksmith, miner, assayer, cattleman, farmer, mechanic, and animal doctor. His long-time friend, Erle Stanley Gardner, who frequently came to his Desert Queen Ranch for visits, compared him to a busy beaver. Bill was a man who enjoyed work. He seemed to have no limits to his energy, even though he worked many times with only his bare hands or with a block and tackle. Whether he was moving a heavy rock or a piece of needed equipment, he steadily plugged along against the force of gravity. Although his methods were sometimes slow, he usually accomplished whatever task he had set out to do. Primarily, this was due to his careful pre-planning of all projects and his tenacious determination to see a job through.

The long hours that he put in each day around his ranch, his mines, or his millsite, became his lifestyle. He had a lot to accomplish, and he hated to waste even a minute of his time when something constructive could be done. This had been his way for as long as he could remember.

The water tanks had been filling for almost an hour when Bill thought he heard the sound of a vehicle in the distance. Stopping work, he walked the seventy-five feet or so up the slope to his millsite for a better view. As he passed through the thick clumps of mesquite growing on the hillside, he was careful not to catch any of his clothing on its thorns. Beneath his feet several Gambel's quail scurried from their cover, only to disappear again into the underbrush.

At the top of the slope was his two-stamp mill. Thirteen years before he had hauled its heavy timbers, belts, and machinery by wagon from Pinyon Wells, set it up here, and renamed it the Wall Street. With its two steel stamps, each weighing more than one thousand pounds, rock ore could be crushed, and its gold extracted by the method of water and mercury. Smaller than the five-stamp mill back at his Desert Queen Ranch, the Wall Street worked well in processing not only his own ore from the Desert Queen Mine, but also that from other area mines as well.

Through the years Bill continued to charge five dollars a ton for providing this service. During busy times when other mines were active, it was not uncommon for his mill to run

4

non-stop night and day with Bill relying on others for temporary help. Sometimes his brothers-in-law, his friend, Oran Booth, or the miners whose ore was being crushed, would take a shift at the amalgam table so that the machinery could continue to run non-stop. With the heavy stamps dropping loudly ninety times a minute, four tons of ore could be processed in twenty-four hours. Down the slope next to the well was a bunkhouse which provided the workmen with beds, cooking facilities and a place to shower.

From the top of the slope, Bill gazed out across a lush landscape of Joshua trees, Mojave yuccas, creosote bushes, and rabbit brush. Scattered among this greenery were splashes of yellow—Prince's plumes, goldenbush, and cassia—the last remnants of the spring wildflowers which only a month ago had covered the desert floor.

However, at this moment Bill's attention was not concentrated on the flora. His eyes were searching for the source of the sounds that he had heard. He looked towards his neighbor's property to the south and in the distance saw Bagley's well. Parked next to the well was a truck fitted with a water tank for hauling. "Maybe Bagley is pumping," he thought. He was unable to tell for certain if someone was there, as he heard no further sounds nor detected any movement in the area.

His curiosity satisfied, he retraced his path down the slope to his engine, then turned to his tanks and troughs to check on their progress. Moments after he arrived, the old engine began an irregular cycle, then stopped abruptly. Then, as he had so many times in the past, he began a methodical check. He cranked it and tested the spark on the magneto. Peering inside, he saw that it was barely faint. "That's the trouble spot," he thought to himself. He continued to adjust the magneto for some time before coming to the conclusion that it must be replaced. Taking a screwdriver from his back pocket, he removed the faulty part, determined to obtain a replacement back at his ranch.

It was another short walk to his car. He placed the magneto on the floor, climbed in, and the old Victory

Dodge started right up on the first try. He turned around and headed south down the dirt road toward the Bagley Well—the same way that he had come in earlier that morning. Bill's thoughts were still on the engine when he arrived at the fence line which separated his property from that of his neighbor, Worth Bagley. It was almost a coincidence, he thought, that the San Bernardino and Riverside County boundaries also fell on this same property line.

As he drove through the break in the fence, his attention was caught by an object looming up straight ahead. Driving closer, he could see that a cardboard sign had been attached to a stake and placed squarely in the middle of the road. Unable to read the lettering from that distance, he drove on to within six feet of the cardboard sign, stopped the car and got out, leaving the engine to idle. As he walked closer, Bill read:

"KEYS, THIS IS MY LAST WARNING.
STAY OFF OF MY PROPERTY."

He read the lettering again, slowly taking in its full meaning, then slowly looked up from the sign. He saw nothing. The desert around him was quiet. Suddenly a noise startled him from his intense concentration. Looking up, he saw a grey bird flying from the top of a nearby Joshua tree. He recognized it as a shrike but his thoughts turned back immediately to the problem at hand. He studied the terrain to his right and left. Still there was no sound or movement. He then walked straight ahead to a small rise where he would be able to get a better view of the surrounding area.

As he was about halfway up the incline, he saw a man coming down to meet him. Although the man was stooped over, Bill recognized him at once. It was his neighbor, Worth Bagley, and he had a gun in his hand! Bill stopped abruptly while Bagley continued to walk towards him. Then almost as sudden as his appearance, Bagley's arm left his side and the gun was pointed directly at Bill. Seeing this, Bill turned equally as fast and ran back to his car. He reached in, grabbed his rifle and stepped aside. At that moment, Bagley fired.

* * * * *

Bill Keys had traveled many roads before fate brought him down the one to his confrontation with Worth Bagley on that day in May, 1943. He was born on the 27th of September, 1879, and began his life with the name of George Barth. His actual birthplace is still a matter of speculation, as even his California family knew little of his early history. However, in his later years, he revealed that he had been born in Russia while his German-born parents were working there as millers. The young Barth family soon emigrated to the United States, settling in Hitchcock County, Nebraska. Here on the banks of Stinkingwater Creek where his parents operated their own grinding mill, the family increased to nine children.

However, George Barth was not to remain in Nebraska. When he was about fifteen years of age he left home, traveling through New Mexico and Arizona, taking a variety of short term jobs along the way. The years passed quickly and he later accepted a position on a cattle drive to Denver, where he had his first taste of big city life. He remained there for several months, then, with some of his former trail buddies, he returned south to Phoenix. Here he became acquainted with Bucky O'Neal, who was recruiting men for Teddy Roosevelt's Rough Riders.

O'Neal's enthusiasm, as well as their own thirst for adventure, convinced George and his friends to enlist. Many took new names, and it was at this time that George Barth became William Key. Just before the group's departure, the potential enlistee became seriously ill and was hospitalized. Upon his release from the hospital several weeks later, the nineteen-year-old discovered that O'Neal, his buddies, and his chance of becoming a Rough Rider had ridden on without him!

During the next three years, William Key drifted across Arizona, stopping long enough to work in the mines of Jerome, then moving on to the George Briggs cattle ranch near Needles, California. Later, he worked for the Conard-Knight Cattle Company near Kingman and served as a deputy sheriff there in 1901 and 1902 in the Arizona Territory.

While working for George Conard, his real education concerning cattle and gunfire began. On one occasion, he and Conard were taking supplies to one of the ranch's outlying line cabins, when they discovered that the building had been taken over and claimed by determined homesteaders. Refusing to leave, the homesteaders opened fire on the ranch wagon, wounding Conard. Key saved his employer's life by pulling him under the wagon, then trading their supplies for his boss's life. After he had unloaded his supplies, he put Conard in the wagon and drove with all possible speed back to the home ranch where Conard was then provided with the much needed medical attention. When Conard and Knight sold out, Key moved on to accept a job at the nearby Gold Roads Mine.

It was at some point during his year with the Gold Roads Mine that he decided to concentrate his future efforts in mining. With several friends, he set out prospecting and developing a number of claims including the Keystone Mine, where he crossed paths with Walter Scott. With a grubstake and seven burros, Death Valley Scotty, as he would later be known, was on his way to fame and fortune in Death Valley. They met again the following year in 1904, when they became better acquainted; however, both men continued to go their separate ways in search of a rich strike. During this time Bill's prospecting included the areas around Goldfield, Rhyolite, Tonopah, Bullfrog, Searchlight, and Quartzite.

Two years later, in 1906, Bill again crossed paths with Scotty. It was at this time they became involved in the infamous Battle of Wingate Pass south of Death Valley. This scheme, cooked up by Scotty, was to sell a gold mine which he did not have to a group of Eastern capitalists. At the last minute he got cold feet and decided to back out of the scheme. In order to scare off the arrival of the investing party and their discovery of the bogus gold mine, Scotty decided to stage a fake ambush. Bill Key was one of the two men whom he enlisted to shoot at the advancing party.

Unfortunately for Scotty, the scheme backfired. By the time the group arrived in Wingate Pass, Bill's companion was drunk and his aim impaired. As a result, Scotty's older brother, Warner, was accidentally but seriously wounded in the blaze of gunfire. The scheme was quickly realized and the trio was arrested several days later and brought to trial in San Bernardino. When it was discovered that the shooting had actually taken place just a few hundred yards inside Inyo County, the charges were dismissed. The frustrated capitalists returned to the East and as a result, Inyo County dropped all charges against the men.

Released from jail, Bill returned to prospecting in the Death Valley area. In a short while, other Easterners approached him with plans to buy and further develop several of his claims. After they had been thoroughly investigated by qualified engineers, the deal was set, the claims were purchased, and the Key Gold Mining Company was formed. Bill took his payment in company stock and traveled back to Boston with company officials. He remained in Boston several months, anxiously watching the value of his stock rise and waiting for exactly the right moment to sell. Unfortunately he waited too long—when the stock took a sudden drop, he lost about $80,000.

His fortune lost, Bill Key returned to California to start over once again, this time south of Death Valley in the Randsburg area and at China Ranch. Throughout 1908 and 1909 he prospected, wandering the desert areas and part of the High Sierra.

By January 1910 he found himself in Barstow. Several days later he drifted south to Old Woman Springs where in the company of other prospectors, he was given an introduction to the area terrain. After working a nearby claim, he headed east to Surprise Spring and later prospected for several months in the Bullion Mountains north of Twentynine Palms. The remainder of the year, he returned to his former skills as a cowboy for one of the cattle companies operating in the area.

In 1911, with his savings from the cattle work, Bill was able to lease the Tully Mine in what is now Joshua Tree National Monument. When he brought his first ore in to a Twentynine Palms stamp mill for crushing, he caused some excitement. It was assayed at $190 a ton! Unfortunately the vein soon played out. He then found work as a watchman and assayer at the nearby Desert Queen Mine.

Remaining on the job for several years, he took care of the mine, its machinery, and the millsite, even when the owning company ceased to be profitable and all mining activity had stopped. As a result, William Morgan, owner of the Desert Queen, found that he owed Bill considerable back wages. Being short of funds himself at this time, he offered Bill the mine and millsite as payment. His offer was readily accepted, for Bill had learned to love the desert.

The Desert Queen millsite was located about six miles from the mine in an isolated canyon almost completely surrounded by high walls of quartz monzonite granite. Here a stream ran following late summer and winter rains. The deed to the millsite included five acres, a five-stamp crushing mill, an adobe barn and several other adobe buildings dating back to the 1890's, at which time the McHaney brothers had operated a cattle ranch at the site. Bill increased his land holdings to eighty acres in 1916 by filing on them as a homestead. In the meantime he built a wooden house with a stone chimney. It was here he brought his bride, Frances Mae Lawton, after their wedding in October, 1918. Together, using patience, ingenuity, and hard work, Bill and Frances built a life for themselves, raised a family of five children, and coped with the harsh realities of desert living.

A decade later, when confusion arose over the similarity of his name with that of a newly arrived homesteader, Bill added an "s" to his last name. The transformation from George Barth to William Keys was now complete.

Bill understood the value of water for survival in an arid land, but the existing wells and a small lake left by the mining company proved inadequate for the needs of the growing Keys family. Through the years additional wells were dug, and windmills and pumps installed. The small rain-fed lake was expanded by the addition of high concrete walls which raised its level as well as its holding capacity.

From this small lake ran irrigation pipes carrying water to their garden and orchard below.

Here, most of the family's food was grown. Later it was processed in jars for winter's use. These canning operations consumed many weeks of activity by the entire family during the hot summer months. Additional supplies and items that could not be grown at the ranch were purchased in Banning and Indio, their nearest towns in the early days. These trips were very infrequent. As a result, family members learned to be self-reliant, to make do with what they had, and to take pride in their independence.

The Keys raised cattle for their own needs, as well as for market, and these animals were responsible for many of Bill's conflicts with others. When he homesteaded his ranch, part of it had been used as a cow camp by the Barker and Shay Cattle Company as far back as the early 1900's. Bill's fences put an end to their continued use of the camp. This caused a succession of conflicts with them, including a gunfight with one of their cowboys and two court cases.

Bill's cattle found a rich variety of grass for pasture in the mountain valleys surrounding his property. Through the years the family had moved their herd to the lower valleys in the fall and to the higher ones in the spring. When most of these areas were included within the newly created Joshua Tree National Monument in 1936, Bill found himself in violation of federal law by continuing his long-established practice.

Bill Keys was not a man who was easily intimidated, even by the United States government, who he felt was wrong in taking so much open land and prohibiting its further use to cattlemen and miners. Now, seven years after the establishment of the Monument, Bill continued to move his cattle twice a year as before, despite numerous warnings. Finally, in order to put an end to the mountain of bureaucratic paperwork involved and also the public embarrassment, the National Park Service agreed to issue him a limited grazing permit. By this time, Bill was the last landowner within the Monument who still had cattle. The Park Service was anxious for a settlement, but their latest permit, due to its wording, had been returned to them unsigned. The Superintendent thought Bill was simply stalling. Perhaps he was, with the hope that the government would just give up and allow him to return to the way of life that had been his for over thirty-three years. However, as no working agreement had yet been reached, Bill's cattle were grazing in Queen Valley for the summer. A well located about three miles from his Desert Queen Ranch provided them with water. It was to fill these tanks and troughs that Bill Keys had driven earlier that morning of May 11, 1943, and thus the biggest controversy of his life began.

* * * * *

Constable Jack Cones had been busy in his office all morning trying to catch up on his backlog of paperwork which he had come to discover was an important part of his job. Twentynine Palms was still a small town, but the large desert surrounding it was also within his jurisdiction. When he wasn't out rounding up lawbreakers, he was many times called upon to search for, and to rescue stranded motorists on the multitude of sandy roads crisscrossing the desert area. Other times he volunteered his services to drive the community ambulance to the nearest hospital, which was in San Bernardino about ninety miles away.

On rare occasions when things were quiet, he would find time to go home for lunch and also have time for his paperwork. Today he decided to concentrate on his office work, so he was glad his wife had packed a lunch for him just in case "something came up," as he was used to telling her.

The forty-seven-year-old constable had seen plenty of action during World War I, while he was assigned to a trench mortar battalion in France. Later, Sergeant Cones would serve as a dispatch rider for General John J. Pershing and, on many occasions, had to motorcycle through machine gun, rifle, and shell fire to get through with his dispatches. Even today, many people said that their heavily-built constable was a man without fear.

12

It was this time of active duty during the war which brought him and his wife, Clara, to settle in the desert in 1929. It was believed the dry climate would help Jack regain his health, and like so many others who had come for the same reason, they homesteaded on 160 acres. Theirs was on the northern outskirts of town. His health did improve, but the first two years were rough ones even for Jack, who had grown up during the hard times of Oklahoma.

To provide meat for the cooking pot, Jack constantly proved his good marksmanship by bringing home jackrabbits. Things became better for them in March 1932 when he was appointed constable by the San Bernardino County Board of Supervisors. Since then, his dedication to his job and to the community that he served had paid off, and he had been re-elected to remain in office from that time on. And now Constable Cones finished his lunch and went back to his paperwork—a stack of papers that seemed no smaller than when he had first started.

*   *   *   *   *

Dave Poste was busy at the switchboard when Bill Keys came into his office at the end of the Twentynine Palms Plaza around 2:45 that afternoon. Dave and his wife, Anna, had been the first telephone operators when the exchange was started in 1936 with a total of four telephones. Besides being the local agent for the California Water and Telephone Company, he was also the current Justice of the Peace.

Dave looked away from his switchboard for a moment and motioned for Bill to have a seat. A few moments later, he covered the mouthpiece of his headset and turning to greet his visitor said, "I'll be right with you, Bill."

Bill nodded and took a chair next to the wall, silently waiting for Dave to finish. His brown eyes wandered around the small room until Dave's voice snapped his attention back to the reason for his visit.

"What's on your mind, Bill?"

"I had a gunfight with Worth Bagley," came his surprising

13

reply. The Magistrate immediately stopped what he was doing and left his seat at the switchboard to take a chair next to Bill.

"Tell me what happened," he said.

Slowly Bill recounted the events of the morning, starting with his pumping water for his cattle, and continuing through Bagley's coming at him with his revolver drawn and firing at him.

"Then I went back to my car, got my rifle and fired back at him. I aimed at his gun hand."

"Did you hit him in his hand?" Dave asked as he leaned over towards Bill.

"I don't know . . . then I fired two more shots. Bagley fell and groaned, then lay still."

"Is Bagley dead?"

"I'm pretty sure he must be, because I watched, and he didn't move."

Bill continued his story, recounting Bagley's movements or "tactics," as he called them, of jumping back and forth as he ran along the hillside just prior to being hit. Dave straightened up in his chair, pondering what he had just heard. Then in a few moments he said, "Well, I guess we had better call the proper authorities. Are you surrendering to me?"

"Yes . . . that's what I came for."

Judge Poste returned to his seat at the switchboard. He put on his headset, reached into the base of the console and pulled out one of the many wires before plugging it into the board. Moments later, he reached an operator.

"Get me a line through to San Bernardino, please—and connect me with Sheriff Shay's office. It's urgent." Then he waited silently.

Several minutes passed before the call went through, then the Justice of the Peace briefly recounted the highlights of the shooting. Completing this call, he immediately placed a call to Jack Cones. He told him of the shooting and stated that Bill Keys was there waiting for him. Cones told him that he would be right over.

"I guess I'd better get in touch with Walt Ketchum,"

stated Dave, "since the shooting occurred in the Monument." As he was about to call the Park Service Headquarters, Bill spoke up.

"Dave, would you also call Frank Bagley? I stopped at his store earlier but he was out. I want to ask him to post my bond."

"Sure thing, Bill." Then he turned back to his switchboard while Bill Keys sat quietly, waiting for the arrival of the constable.

*   *   *   *   *

Everything was ready. The refreshments were made, the coffee was simmering in the kitchen, and arrangements had been made for Ada Hatch to pour. The chairs were all in place in the large living room, the "No Smoking" signs were out on every table, and her house was immaculate. Today Betty Campbell was sponsoring a cultural event for her guests—the Twentynine Palms Women's Club.

It was almost two o'clock. She looked at her watch, as she heard sounds of automobiles pulling into the driveway of her large two-story house. "Right on time," she thought, as she walked toward the front hallway. More vehicles were arriving and parking under the shade of the large athol trees, as she opened the front door and began greeting her guests. One of the first to arrive was the club's president, Mrs. Roman. She was followed by the club's secretary, who, after greeting Mrs. Campbell, took her seat at a table by the door. The arriving ladies showed their membership cards, spoke to their hostess, then passed through the door into the hallway. Within ten minutes more than seventy-five women had filed into the living room to take their seats for the meeting.

While they were waiting for the last members to arrive and for the start of the meeting, many of those in the room glanced around, noting the elegance of its furnishings. The many antique pieces, the heavy curtain rods with pulls, the glass-doored bookcases built on each side of the fireplace, and the beautiful rugs were items that no one missed seeing.

15

Another rare sight was the highly polished hardwood floors. Desert heat and dryness made such floors impractical in the area, not to mention the expense which put such luxuries out of the reach of most of those in the room. They all knew that Betty Campbell had inherited money from her family, and that her house had been built to her design and modeled after the Pennsylvania farmhouse where she had been reared.

Another item which surely did not escape the notice of anyone were the "No Smoking" signs prominently displayed on the tables around the room. No one dared mention these signs nor did they dare disregard them! It wasn't every day that Betty Campbell invited so many people as guests into her home. Weeks earlier, invitations had been sent out, and there had been a scurry to find long lost hats and gloves for this special occasion.

The meeting was soon called to order. After the club's business was concluded, Betty Campbell stepped forward to introduce her special guests. Coming from the back of the room, as she called their names, were Charles Harwell and John Baker from the National Audubon Society.

Baker, the Society's executive secretary, spoke of their rapidly growing membership, after which Charles Harwell took his place at the grand piano. Part of his program consisted of asking the audience to identify the different bird calls that he would produce on the keyboard. Most of the ladies correctly recognized the calls of the local desert varieties, then Mr. Harwell turned his attention to his hostess.

"Mrs. Campbell, can you tell me the name of this bird?"

"I'll try," came her cautious reply. She listened as the well-turned notes were sounded. "Why, that's a cuckoo," she replied.

This brought a laugh from the audience as Harwell said, "You're right! Now who can name this next one?"

Suddenly the sound of birds was interrupted by the shrill ring of the telephone on the landing above the stairway. Their hostess excused herself. The heels of the large woman clattered on the polished wooden floor as she left the room and started towards the stairs. She quickly stepped over the "No Trespassing" signs which barred entrance to this area of her house and continued up to the landing.

Everything suddenly became quiet as Betty's loud voice carried to all parts of the room. Due to poor hearing, her speaking voice was much louder than normal. As a result, her guests sat quietly, clearly hearing her side of the conversation and awaiting completion of the call.

"Is that right, Mr. Poste? Oh, I'll get Mr. Ketchum immediately." Quickly retracing her steps, she again climbed over the sign and returned to her guests. "Mr. Ketchum, you're wanted on the telephone."

Walt Ketchum, the Assistant Custodian or Superintendent of Joshua Tree National Monument was the only man present and had been especially invited by Mrs. Campbell to attend today's presentation. He left his chair in the corner and walked to the stairway landing to take his call. He returned quickly, grabbed his hat and prepared to leave.

"Ladies, please excuse me. Worth Bagley's been shot and killed and I must go up to his ranch." Without another word, he was out of the house, into his car, and heading towards town to meet Jack Cones.

Mr. Harwell returned to his program, while his audience sat quietly wondering what had happened and wishing this meeting of the Women's Club would quickly end.

*   *   *   *   *

When Jack Cones' car drove up in front of Dr. Gilbert Leonard's office, Dave Poste was seated beside him while Bill Keys sat in the back seat. They remained in the car while Cones went into the office. He returned a few minutes later with the doctor, and just as they were getting into the vehicle, Walt Ketchum drove up.

"Walt, you ride with the Doc," said the constable. "The two of you can follow us."

The cars headed south from the Plaza to the Four Corners' stop sign, then turned east onto the main highway. About one mile further, they turned right and headed south up the hill into Joshua Tree National Monument. The paved road shortly gave way to dirt. However, the two cars continued to move along with hardly a change in pace even though they were quickly enveloped in a cloud of dust. Despite the growing use by Monument visitors, most of the roads were in no better condition now than when they were used by miners' ore wagons in the 1890's.

The road climbed higher, winding past the abandoned Anaconda mine, the Split Rock formation, the Jumbo Rocks, and the turnoff to the aircraft watchtower, before finally coming out into Queen Valley. Here on this high plateau, it leveled off at an elevation of 2,500 feet higher than that of Twentynine Palms. The occupants of the two cars could also feel the difference in air temperature, as it was approximately ten degrees cooler at this elevation.

Constable Cones slowed his speed. He watched anxiously for the side road which would be their turning point, taking them the last three miles to the Bagley ranch. Along both sides of this road through Queen Valley, Mojave mound and beavertail cacti were beginning to show their colors in the May heat. If the occupants of the cars noticed this desert beauty, they made no comment, for each rode silently listening to his own thoughts.

The lead car slowed still further as it made a right turn with the doctor's car still following. Then at 4:20, they reached the cattleguard and fork in the road just outside the Bagley fence. From here they could see the well directly beyond the fence with the water truck still parked beside it. About a quarter mile directly west of the well was the ranch house.

"That road over there is the one we want," said Bill, pointing to the right. "We don't have to go into the main part of the ranch at all. Bagley's just up the road a piece."

The cars turned away from the cattleguard to follow the sandy road that paralleled the two-strand barbed wire fence for a short distance. Suddenly, Cones swerved to avoid hitting some broken glass lying in his path, then immediately pulled back into the deep sandy ruts that marked the road. "Bagley did that!" Bill said excitedly.

A few minutes later the constable's car came to an abrupt halt. They could all see Bagley lying in the brush just a few feet west of the car. He was face down in the sand. The cars pulled off the roadway into the brush, and the men got out. Cones took immediate charge of the party and gave his first order.

"Everyone but Doc Leonard stay clear of the body and the area around it. Keep to the east side of the roadway, so we don't destroy any footprints or other evidence."

The doctor moved carefully towards the body, stepping over it to begin his preliminary examination. The others watched silently from the edge of the roadway. He looked closely at Bagley's left arm, which was positioned above his head. It was badly mutilated and appeared to have been almost severed at the elbow. His right hand was up close to his face and held a Colt .38 calibre revolver. His grip was still firmly wrapped around the butt, and his index finger extended over the trigger. It was cocked.

Doctor Leonard reached over, grasped Bagley's left leg, and tested it for tension. Then he bent down close to the head, raised an eyelid, and checked the pupil.

"He's dead all right," he announced to the group. Continuing his examination, he noticed a wound above the right elbow. There was also some blood on his shirt in the area of his lower back. Carefully, he tore away several inches of the shirt to expose the wound more fully.

While the doctor was concentrating on the body, the other four men turned from their silent vigil and started down the slope toward the fence marking the Bagley property line.

"Back by this Joshua tree . . . that's where I fired," Bill said, walking to the spot where he had stood earlier that morning.

The constable didn't have to ask too many questions, as Bill was eager to tell the men what had happened. He walked through the opening in the fenceline, stopped, then turned around to face them.

"Here's my property in San Bernardino County, and over there," he said, pointing beyond them, "where Bagley fell, is in Riverside County." Then he turned and pointed to the Joshua tree again. "This tree's the county dividing line. I put that old sign up here years ago to mark the beginning of my land." Pointing east, he added, "Over there about forty feet or so is the section marker which is in line with this tree."

Walking over behind the Joshua tree, he continued. "So anyway, I was stopped by this Joshua tree. I had left the engine running and opened the door so that I could walk over and read that sign sticking up over there." The men looked at the cardboard sign which was still in place, as he continued. "Then I started up that rise over there for a look-see. When I was part way up and could just see over the top, I saw Bagley. He was bending over some dead Joshua trees and coming toward me in this crouched position," he said, demonstrating. "When I saw he had a gun in his right hand, I turned, went back to my car, reached in and got my rifle."

The other men looked in the direction of the rise, as Bill spoke. Each was trying to visualize the events as they were related.

"Bagley fired when he got to the top of the rise. I don't know where that bullet went, but it was close—somewhere between me and my car. When I fired at his gun hand, he took off running—kinda zigzag-like. Then I fired twice more in rapid succession. My third shot brought him down."

Cones asked Bill a few more questions before he and the others returned to where Doc Leonard was waiting. The doctor stood up as they approached, then spoke directly to Cones. "Looks like death was instantaneous . . . probably the bullet in the side did him in. Of course, it will take a more thorough examination by someone who specializes in that sort of thing, to determine that for sure."

Cones considered the doctor's verdict. "Thanks, Doc. If you're all finished, I think we can leave. I need to get down to the junction in case the coroner and the county deputies get there." With that, the group headed back toward the cars.

As they started off, Bill walked next to the constable. "Oh, I picked up two of the shells I fired. You'll find them in the front seat of my car down in Twentynine Palms. I couldn't find the third one." He then dropped back beside Dave Poste, walked silently for a few paces, considering the request he was about to make. After a few more moments hesitation, he spoke. "Dave, would you do me a favor and turn my car over to Karl Schapel when he stops by to see you. Earlier this afternoon, I asked him to watch my place while I'm gone, and he agreed. Here's the key," he said, handing it to the Magistrate. "Karl can use it while he's up at the ranch."

"Sure, I'll take care of it for you," Poste said just as they reached the parked cars. Poste got into the doctor's car with Walt Ketchum while Bill got in with Jack. Cones' car started immediately, turned around, and headed south along the road on which they had come.

Just as he was about to turn left at the cattleguard, Jack glanced into his rear view mirror. He noticed that the other car had stopped. He slowed down, keeping one eye on the mirror to see if the doctor's car was moving. It still had not moved by the time he reached the junction, so he stopped his car.

"Maybe they're stuck," he theorized to Bill, "but let's walk back there to see what's the trouble, anyway."

They got out and began the return trip on foot along the dirt road. Suddenly they saw the doctor's car starting towards them. Seconds later, as it reached their position, Dave Poste spoke to them through the open window.

"We got stuck in the sand."

"Just as I thought," Cones answered. "We're going to wait here awhile to see that the county deputies don't miss this turn and end up in the ranch. Doc, if you see them on your way back to town, tell them we're waiting here."

"Sure thing, Jack."

With that, Keys and Cones returned to their car and watched as the doctor's car and its three passengers pulled around them and headed east, disappearing from view. The two men sat there silently waiting for a glimpse of an approaching car. It was several minutes before either of them spoke. Cones finally broke the silence. "Let's take a

21

look at that water truck over there at the well. It'll help kill a little time."

They walked directly toward the cattleguard marking the entrance through the barbed wire fence into the main part of the Bagley ranch.

"I built this fence with four other men to try and satisfy Bagley's complaint about my trespassing cattle," said Bill. As they passed through the fenceline, he pointed towards the well. "That truck wasn't there this morning when I first drove up to my pump, but it's sure got a heavy load on it now."

They walked around the old truck, looking it over, when Jack asked, "I wonder how much water there is in it?"

Without a moment's hesitation, Bill stepped closer to the tank, tapped its side, then climbed up onto the truck's body and looked inside. "It's almost full," he called down. He then jumped from the truck and rejoined the constable. They both leaned against the vehicle in silence.

Jack's eyes scanned the roadway for a sign of dust signalling an approaching vehicle, but the horizon was clear. His impatience growing by the minute, he straightened up and started to walk away from the truck.

"Well, let's go, Bill. Maybe we'll find them out on the main road."

Minutes later their car was headed east, following the same route as the doctor's, and approached the main Monument road. Reaching the junction, they pulled off the road's edge, shut off the engine and waited.

* * * * *

Anna Poste was working the switchboard when Doctor Leonard dropped her husband off on his return from the Bagley ranch. Dave brought her up to date on the events of the afternoon, in particular the story of the shooting. He mentioned Bill's request, and the two of them stepped outside of their office to find Bill's car still parked where it had been left earlier. They saw that the old Victory Dodge was still in remarkably good shape. Its body showed few scars of any type, and its paint, although showing effects of the harsh desert wind and sun, was in good condition. Together they walked around it, their eyes searching for any sign that might have been made by Bagley's bullet.

Their first examination revealed nothing. Then Anna opened the door on the driver's side and looked inside. Her gaze passed across the empty rifle cartridges lying on the front seat. She looked closer at the area surrounding the door frame, and her attention was drawn to an odd-shaped mark.

"Dave, come here and look at this."

Her husband passed quickly around the vehicle to see what his wife had discovered. She pointed to a half-moon scar about seven inches below the door handle in the thin strip that covered the door jamb.

"Well, what do you think about this?"

He bent down closer to look at the dent, which was about the size of his fingertip.

"Yes, it could have been made by a bullet," Dave agreed. "There are little bits of silver metal still clinging around the hole. They could be lead fragments." Dave knew better than to destroy possible evidence, so he got up and carefully closed the door. "We'll report this to Jack when he comes down later," he said. With that, he and Anna walked back into their office to resume their regular duties.

* * * * *

Cones and his prisoner had been waiting about fifteen minutes when they spotted a swirl of dust moving westward along the road. In a few minutes they saw a government vehicle, and as it pulled up next to them, they recognized Duane Jacobs seated behind the wheel. The Acting Custodian of the Monument idled his engine as he spoke to them through his open window.

"Hello, Jack. What's going on? Mrs. Poste called and said that you were trying to reach me."

23

"Yes, there's been a shooting over at the Bagley place."

"There sure was," interrupted Bill, "and I got him! He's over there on the road to my mill."

"You'd better join us, Duane," invited the constable.

"Sure. Let me park this first, and I'll be right with you." The ranger pulled his car onto the shoulder of the road, walked back to the other car, opened the door and got into the back seat.

"We're waiting here for the Sheriff's men from San Bernardino. There are so many roads up here, they've probably made a wrong turn and got lost," theorized Jack.

It's an easy thing to do. I've been here six months and haven't been on all of these back roads either," Jacobs admitted.

The three men talked among themselves while they waited. Bill and Jacobs were outwardly friendly to each other, but there was no great friendship here. Like his predecessor, Duane Jacobs had found Bill to be a stubborn man. He was determined to enforce the established government regulations and hoped that Bill would quickly sign his grazing permit so that legal proceedings would not be necessary. The National Park Service also wanted access to the lake at Barker Dam; the only way was through Bill Keys' property. So far, this access had been denied. They had threatened to cut the locks on his gate, if this continued.

Bill, on the other hand, felt that the government had made a mistake in taking so much open land and locking it up for city sightseers when it could be more productively used for grazing and mining. He had written to Washington officials on several occasions expressing his viewpoint about the waste of manpower, gas, and rubber that was being used to administer the Monument—especially now during war times. He had said, "An old man can take care of a monument like this one out here in the desert—there is no physical labor to do." Also, he had not forgotten the threat made by Jacob's predecessor, Jim Cole, who had intimated to him and his wife, Frances, that the government could start condemnation proceedings against them. They would lose their ranch, if they weren't cooperative.

"We have ways unknown to you of getting you out of here," Cole had told them as they sat in the living room during one of his visits. Since that time, Bill's dislike for the National Park Service had remained unchanged.

The trio hadn't long to wait before the missing deputies arrived. Walt Ketchum was driving. With him were County Deputies Harry Heap, Perry Green, and William Russell. As their car stopped opposite Cones', Russell got out, crossed the roadway, and got into the back seat. At this point, Duane Jacobs returned to his own vehicle.

"You follow us, Ketch," the constable said, starting off before Ketchum had time to do any more than nod in agreement.

Jacobs' government car became the third one in the procession that headed back across the edge of Queen Valley to the scene of the shooting.

"Mr. Keys, this is Bill Russell from the San Bernardino County Sheriff's office," said Jack, as he introduced the two men. Then he gave the arriving deputy a brief summary of the shooting.

Bill sat quietly in the front seat, listening to the two lawmen's discussion. Then Russell leaned over the seat and inquired, "What's this trouble all about, Mr. Keys? What led up to this shooting?"

"Well, I've been losing cattle for some time now—even found some shot with a .22 rifle. I've still got the bullets as evidence and even went down to Riverside to complain. Then, just yesterday, one of my mares disappeared. I think Bagley was behind these problems."

Bill briefly related the events of the morning for Russell. "After Bagley fired at me, and I fired back, he started running and zigzagging. He probably thought his police tactics could outmaneuver my aim." As Bill was talking, the three cars arrived at the road junction near the Bagley well. Cones interrupted to speak to Russell.

"Before we get to the body, I want to show you something in the road over there."

Jack slowed his car to a stop and got out, telling the men in the other cars to follow him. A few yards away, he pointed

25

out the broken glass lying in the roadway. The deputies grouped around him and two of them bent down to examine the glass more closely. "It appears to be pieces of a five-gallon jug," one of them commented.

"Bagley must have put that there after I drove through," Bill answered. "It wasn't there when I drove to my pump early this morning."

Russell and Green picked up the glass and put it near the barbed wire fence before rejoining the others at the cars. Then they made the short drive north towards the shooting site. Several hundred feet from the body, Cones once again stopped and got out, followed by the others. The group stopped near the two apparent rock and log barricades which partially blocked the roadway.

Deputy Heap knelt at one of them and examined the ground. "There's only one set of tire tracks going beyond here, and they appear to have been made before this barricade was put in place. See, the logs are placed over the tracks," he said, pointing to them.

As the men walked around the barricade, a sign and a hammer lying at the base of a Joshua tree caught their attention. A hundred feet further, the men saw Bagley's body lying at the side of the roadway, partially obscured by a clump of blackbrush. North of the body was another sign—the one that Bill had seen just before the shooting began. Its wording was identical to that on the sign they had just seen at the base of the Joshua tree.

Russell and his men looked briefly at the body, while Bill stood by silently. His silence was to be short-lived, for once again he was asked to repeat all of the events of the morning, starting from the very beginning. As he talked and pointed out different locations, the group moved down the road toward the Joshua tree near his property line. From here he had fired the three shots at Bagley.

In the midst of his testimony, as he glanced toward the ground, something caught his attention. "Here's the missing shell!" he exclaimed. He reached down to retrieve it from the road's edge and handed it to Russell, who glanced at it before dropping it into his pocket.

Bill resumed his story, pointing out the survey stake, then he spoke of the actual shooting. "After I got my rifle out of the car, I aimed at his gun hand. I shot a little high and hit him in the upper right arm. Then Bagley turned to the left like this," he demonstrated, "and started running zigzag-like, using his police tactics. But I fired twice more before he could shoot at me again. It was a case of self-defense."

"Self-defense!" Deputy Heap interrupted. "Why, you shot the man in the back, as he was running!"

"No, I didn't! He was trying to outmaneuver me, but my rifle was an automatic, and it shot fast!" Bill exclaimed.

"So you say!"

"That's enough, Harry," interrupted Bill Russell. "Go on with your story, Mr. Keys."

While this questioning continued, Duane Jacobs left the group and walked east to climb a small rise about forty feet away. Among some clumps of rabbit brush, he discovered the section stake that Keys had mentioned. Bending down to study it closer, he saw that the 2½-inch brass cap was attached to a pipe set firmly in the ground. Across the round cap was written:

U.S. General Land Office
S-34
¼
191

In the meantime, the deputies had walked back to the body with Bill and were studying Bagley's prone, out-stretched position in an attempt to plot his last movements. As his feet were pointed toward the west, the lawmen began searching for his tracks in that direction. Several heavy indentations in the soil attracted their attention.

"His tracks indicate that he came along the slope, made a sharp turn, then headed back towards the roadway for about twenty feet before falling face down in the sand," one of the deputies theorized.

Russell left the men to walk to one of the barricades. He asked Bill to join him. The others followed and a closer look revealed several dead Joshua trees partially pulled into the roadway. Rocks had been piled against them, but it appeared the task had not been completed. "I think Bagley was working on this when my car surprised him," said Bill.

Deputy Heap measured the car tracks just south of the barricade when Bill pointed out, "I drove on the righthand side of the road when I went in. It's rougher there, but I got better traction because of the sand."

Taking a notebook out of his pocket, Russell made a few notes before continuing with his questions. "What time did this shooting take place, Mr. Keys?"

"It was about eleven o'clock."

"Are you sure of that? What time did you get up?"

"Well, I have no clock, but I get up about the same time every morning. Today, I came to pump water, and it's about a fifteen minute trip from my ranch to here. I'd say I got here about nine-thirty."

"And what did you do after the shooting?"

"I backed my car up and took the other road. That's the one that leaves back there by my well and heads out into Queen Valley a bit. From there it turns south, connecting with the main Monument road. It's about five miles further but I took this longer way back to my ranch. When I got home, I fixed the magneto, had something to eat, changed clothes, and came back to the well—again by the long way— and pumped water for about two hours."

"Okay. Is there anything else that you can remember about your return trip to the well?"

"Well, out of curiosity, I came down here near that rise over there to see if I could see anything of Bagley . . . but I didn't go anywhere near the body!"

"Why not?"

"Why, I thought he might still be alive, but I couldn't see anything of him from where I was standing. So, I got into my car and went down to Twentynine Palms to report the shooting to Magistrate Poste."

Russell made a few more notes, writing quickly, while the other deputies stood silently weighing Bill's testimony. When he had finished writing, he looked up. "Why didn't you go down the road the way you had originally driven in?"

28

"There was that sign in the road and these barricades," stated Bill, pointing to the nearby obstructions.

"Oh hell, they're so small, they couldn't have kept any car from going down this road. Are you sure Bagley wasn't shot earlier—say like last night, and someone else put these barricades across the road later?" the deputy intimated coyly.

"No! It didn't happen that way!" came Bill's excited reply. Then he sneered and laughed at this accusation. "No, you've got it all wrong—all wrong."

"Well, from the evidence I've seen, it looks as though Bagley could have been shot while he was on the ground, and the gun put into his hand afterwards. Isn't that possibly the way it happened?" theorized Russell, continuing to look straight at Keys.

"No! I told you how it happened!"

"Did you shoot him from your automobile?"

"No. I was back there by that Joshua tree!" snapped Bill.

And so the questioning continued with the deputies repeating the same questions over and over again, checking and rechecking his story, but Bill remained steadfast with his answers.

Finally, Jack Cones interrupted. "Harry, I'm turning Keys over to your custody now and going to see if I can find the coroner's ambulance." Without waiting for a reply, he walked back to his car, got in and turned around, maneuvering past the others on the narrow dirt road. The car picked up speed as Cones headed south towards the Bagley well, turned left and disappeared into the swirling dust.

*　*　*　*　*

It was well after dark when he returned. Not finding the missing vehicle on the road, Cones had returned to his office and called the Banning substation. On his desk he found a message that Dave Poste wanted to see him. Driving over to the Plaza, he found Poste busy as usual at the switchboard.

29

Anna took over while her husband went outside with Jack to Bill's car. Dave pointed out the marks on the door and asked him to report it to the deputies. "Sure thing, Dave. We'll need this car for evidence, so would you have someone drive it over to Tom Martin's garage and put into storage?" The magistrate agreed and the two men parted.

Jack decided to return once again to the Bagley ranch. On the way he stopped to pick up an order of sandwiches for the men still on duty. The twenty-two-mile return trip was uneventful. When he arrived at the site of the shooting, there was no one there—only Bagley's body, now covered with a blanket and still resting among the desert shrubs where it had fallen. Looking to the west, Cones saw lights at the ranch house and knew where the men were.

Minutes later, he drove over the cattleguard into the fenced area of the ranch, passing the well and parked water truck along the way. The dirt road headed due west for about a quarter mile to the rocky cove where the single story concrete house was located.

Cones opened the porch door that led into the large living room. Here he found not only the deputies that he had met earlier, but others from the Riverside County Sheriff's Office. Bill was now in their custody, as it was believed that Bagley had died in their jurisdiction. A surveyor would be needed to make this determination.

Cones delivered the sandwiches to the hungry lawmen, most of whom had not eaten since lunchtime. As he walked around the room, looking at its contents, a gun rack along the west wall caught his attention. A closer look revealed an old Springfield rifle, a .22, and an air gun. Cones knew that Bagley had been a former deputy in Los Angeles County, and that most people living out here in the desert had firearms. Many times such weapons provided food for the table.

He soon realized there was nothing more he could do. He was tired, the coroner was on his way, and Keys was no longer his responsibility. With these thoughts, he returned to his car and headed back towards Twentynine Palms. About three miles from the ranch, the headlights of an approaching vehicle pierced the darkness. "Must be the coroner," he thought. It slowed down as he approached, and he saw it was the missing ambulance.

Inside, Dave Poste was riding with a man from the coroner's office. "Sorry we're late, Jack, but I got lost showing him the way. I'm still not familiar with all these roads up here, especially in the dark. This afternoon was my first trip to Bagley's. After we get to the ranch, can I ride back to town with you?"

"Sure, Dave," Cones replied. He turned his car and, with the ambulance following, returned to the ranch. While the coroner's vehicle waited near the cattleguard, he drove over to the house to notify the deputies.

Fifteen minutes later, with several of the lawmen helping, the body was placed into the vehicle. It was almost eleven o'clock when its lights finally disappeared down the dirt road to begin the return trip to Banning, and with it, Worth Bagley left his ranch for the last time.

*   *   *   *   *

About an hour and a half later, the ambulance pulled into the side of Weifel's and Son Mortuary, and the stretcher carrying the body was taken inside to the preparation room. When Deputy Coroner Cash began his examination, Bagley was still wearing his cartridge belt and holster. These were removed along with his blue denim trousers and blood-stained shirt. After Cash has finished, Mr. Chapman of the mortuary staff cleansed the body, being careful not to dislodge any debris, powder marks, or other foreign materials from in or around the wounds. He knew that these areas would receive close scrutiny during the full autopsy to be performed later.

This task complete, he embalmed the body, covered it with a sheet, and left with the Deputy Coroner, calling it a day.

*   *   *   *   *

31

Late that evening, the Superintendent of Joshua Tree National Monument sent the following telegram:

May 11, 1943
11:30 P.M.

Regional Director
National Park Service
601 Shelton Building
San Francisco, California

Worth Bagley killed by Keys today in Monument. If grazing permit not already executed recommend no further consideration be given Keys. Will inform you results of investigation by County authorities when available.

Jacobs

* * * * *

It was after midnight when the last lights were extinguished, and the Bagley ranch house was quiet. Over thirteen hours had elapsed since the sound of gunfire had echoed across Queen Valley. Now, a slight southerly wind rustled the sharp-pointed leaves of the yuccas and Joshua trees in the front yard. Behind the house, a great horned owl slipped from its perch into silent flight in search of seed-gathering mice and ground squirrels. Amongst the ground shrubs, a gopher snake was on the same quest. High above the house on a rocky ledge, a restless coyote paced back and forth, calling to its mate. But almost as suddenly as he had begun, his voice was still, and he disappeared into the shadows. Soon the wind also stopped. Then night crept across the desert landscape, enveloping it in gentle silence.

II

May 12, 1943
Wednesday

Bill Keys returned to the shooting site the next morning in the custody of Captain Walwrath and Deputies Mulvey and McCracken from the Riverside County Sheriff's Office. Also on hand were Deputy Coroner Cash and retired Deputy Ben De Crevecour, a man who had made a place for himself in local desert history by leading the posse that had tracked down Willie Boy in 1909.

With these men as witnesses, Bill once again retraced the events of the previous day, pointing out where he and Bagley had been during the entire confrontation. As he talked and moved from one location to another, photographs and measurements were taken between the various points, with the different deputies acting as stand-ins for the principals in the shooting. Today's questioning also had the benefit of Seymer Cash's skill in taking dictation.

Throughout the entire interrogation, Bill remained calm, his story unchanged, but Deputy McCracken seemed unsatisfied with several points.

"Now Mr. Keys, after Bagley dropped, did you go up there?"

"No. I went back toward my mill."

"You mean you didn't go up to see whether he was dead or not?"

"No. I thought he was alive," Bill answered firmly.

"So you didn't know whether you hit him or not?"

"No, I didn't know, but I thought I did. I was shooting on

the run, and he fell, and I cleared out. I didn't know if I hit him fatally or not, but I sure didn't trust going up there to find out."

"Okay, Mr. Keys. Now when you came back from your ranch to your pump yesterday, didn't you feel a little worried?"

"No, not a bit. It didn't make me nervous at all. The shooting was justified. My trough was dry and my cattle were out here. They need water first."

"Well, weren't you worried that he might circle around and bushwack you?"

"No, I kept a close look around the whole time I was pumping."

"Okay. Did you or Bagley have any words before the shooting?"

"No, none at all. I was hoping that he would speak . . . I stood here, and I was hoping that he would, but he didn't. After he shot, I started firing. This has been a public road for a long time, and I have been traveling it all the time."

"All right. One more question. When was the last time you were inside of the cattleguard by the well—that is, inside the Bagley ranch?"

"I haven't been inside there since Bagley moved in here—other than yesterday when I was with Jack Cones and you fellows over at the house."

"And how long would you say that's been?"

"Oh, about three years."

With Bill Keys in Walwrath's custody, McCracken left the others and returned to the Bagley ranch house. He had wanted to look around the previous evening but darkness had hampered his investigation at that time. He was very thorough and paid a great deal of attention to detail. Because of this thoroughness, he had been very successful with his assigned cases.

McCracken slowly walked around the concrete block house. He could see that additional rooms had been added at separate times. Although he guessed that the blocks were probably homemade, the building appeared sound. As he was studying its construction, a sign posted on its northeast side caught his attention. The lettering was large enough to be seen quite clearly:

WARNING. THIS PROPERTY
PROTECTED BY GUNTRAPS

The lawman took note of the warning, as he carefully continued around the house. He had seen similar signs throughout the desert in his almost twenty years with the Sheriff's office, and he didn't take such warnings lightly. Moments later, he was back at the front of the house. After glancing at the contents on the porch, he passed through the front door and entered the house to continue his examination.

*   *   *   *   *

While Deputy McCracken was inside the Bagley house Captain Walwrath, accompanied by Bill Keys, was driving over to Bill's Desert Queen Ranch. Walwrath's goal was to pick up the clothing that Bill had been wearing on the day of the shooting.

The three-mile drive to the ranch took about ten minutes. The dirt road meandered through Joshua trees and piles of high granite boulders before crossing a dry wash and ending in a rock-enclosed canyon that Bill called home. Three hundred yards further it crossed the wash again and climbed up a small rise before dead-ending in front of Bill's house. Between their car and the house was a fence made of Joshua tree logs that had been piled on top of one another. The four-foot-high fence stretched across the front yard, ending at an old adobe barn to their right about two hundred feet away.

Walwrath could see a great deal from where he sat. To the right of the house was an orchard with a dozen or more pear trees. Some still had a few of their blossoms intact. Beyond the trees, the bank sloped down to meet the dry wash that they had just crossed. On its opposite side was the five-stamp crushing mill. Its huge wooden timbers had been there since the 1890's.

The lawman got out of his car and turned to look behind

35

him. To his left and right, he saw several small wooden buildings. Scattered amongst them were organized piles of machinery, mining tools, wire, lumber, pipe, spare parts, and other equipment. Old car bodies, wooden wagons and farm machinery sat next to old-time gas and wood stoves, while piles of automobile tires rested near vacant beehives.

"It was no wonder that Keys came back here to get his magneto fixed," Walwrath thought. "He probably has a spare part for anything he ever used."

As Bill got out of the car, he directed Walwrath toward the house, and the two men walked through the opening in the log fence that passed into the inner yard. The wooden house wasn't large, and Walwrath could easily see that it had been added onto at different times. The outer surface of the wood was splintering from many years of extreme heat and dryness. Its dark brown color was peeking through in places where the green paint had long ago peeled away. The chimney at the end of the house also caught his attention. Its granite stones appeared to have been expertly cut to uniform size, then fitted together into a well-built structure. A metal barrel rested above the opening at its top, probably creating a good draft for the fire, as well as protecting it from inclement weather. "Damn clever," he thought.

The two men disappeared into the house, passing through the front door that led into the small wallpapered living room. Minutes later, they returned with a pair of blue denim trousers, a green jacket, and a pair of boots. Bill had identified them as being the clothes Walwrath sought and had surrendered them willingly. Then, after locking the door, they drove back to the Bagley ranch to rejoin the others still waiting there.

III

May 13, 1943
Thursday

Amos Brown got an early start this morning. He was heading towards the Bagley ranch where he had been assigned to make a survey. This deputy coroner's assignment was to map certain portions of the ranch, as well as the surrounding area, connected with the shooting. His determination of the county boundaries would settle the question of where Worth Bagley had fallen, but this particular mission would take at least two more trips to complete.

* * * * *

Another individual interested in the Keys case was driving towards Riverside. Paul Barksdale D'Orr had been in practice for more than fifteen years, and it was not be chance that Frances Keys had telephoned him the previous day. The experienced lawyer had been associated with the Keys family since 1930, when he had defended Bill against the charges brought by a cowboy from an influential cattle family in San Bernardino County. D'Orr had been brilliant in that celebrated case. He had easily proven Bill's innocence in a conflict which had also resulted in gunfire. Since that time, he had represented the family interests in their many mining claims and other transactions necessitating legal expertise.

About an hour and a half after leaving his home in Los Angeles, the middle-aged attorney arrived at the Riverside

37

County jail. After parking his car, he went inside to meet once again with his old friend and to plan his defense against the charges that the Riverside County District Attorney was preparing.

* * * * *

Shortly before 5:00 P.M., Dr. Frank R. Webb rounded the corner onto Nicolet Street and pulled into the parking area of Wiefels and Son Mortuary in Banning. The doctor had performed more than thirty thousand autopsies since beginning with Los Angeles County in 1917. Now, as its Chief Autopsy Surgeon, he didn't expect this evening's work to be any different from so many other shooting cases that he had been called upon to examine personally.

As he walked through the mortuary's double glass doors, he was met by Riverside surgeon Wayne Templeton. Together they went down the hallway to the preparation room. Here Mr. Chapman greeted the doctors, leading them to the examining table where the body of Worth Bagley lay. After removing the covering sheet, he stepped back, allowing the two doctors to begin.

They worked quickly and efficiently, almost routinely, first making a survey of the general appearance of the nude body that lay before them. Their attention was drawn to the muscles of Bagley's left forearm, which were smaller and not as well developed as those on his right.

"Looks like he had a bad injury here years ago," Webb pointed out.

His companion nodded, then commented, "From the condition of the body, I'd say it had been exposed for at least twelve hours before Chapman embalmed it."

Webb agreed, then, reaching for a scalpel, opened the body cavity to begin the thorough examination. A few minutes later, they concluded that the heart and other vital organs were normal for a man they estimated to be about forty-five years of age. Their attention then concentrated on the probable cause of death. The left forearm appeared to have been shattered by a gunshot which had fragmented

38

both bones and torn the muscles into shreds. The skin of the right arm had also sustained a wound about three inches above the elbow. The third wound, however, appeared to be the most serious. It was on Bagley's left side about fifteen inches below shoulder level. Here was the bullet's entrance into the body cavity. As they traced its upward movement, a damaging path was revealed. After locating the metal projectile, they set it aside to be turned over to the Coroner's office.

As a result of their examination, they both concluded that this same bullet had probably shattered the left arm before continuing on through Bagley's left side; that death was due to hemorrhage; and that shock was probably instantaneous.

Their work completed, they washed up and departed, leaving Mr. Chapman to prepare the body of Worth Bagley for the pending burial services.

IV

May 14, 1943
Friday

It took only a few minutes for the two men to walk across the street from the Riverside jail and to pass into an adjacent building. The lawman directed the man in his charge into one of the offices. As Bill Keys entered, he immediately recognized the thirty-two-year-old District Attorney seated at his desk. He also recognized Seymer Cash seated to his right.

After Bill was directed to a chair in front of the D.A.'s desk, Neblett spoke. "Mr. Keys—on Tuesday morning, what time did you leave your ranch?"

"Well, the San Bernardino County officers already had about thirty-five or forty men questioning me, and my attorney said I shouldn't talk too much."

"Okay, but you remember, I talked to you out there Tuesday night for a little while?"

"I think so," answered Bill.

"Well, you told us what happened. Now, I just want to go over that again, while Mr. Cash is here—to fix it in my own mind. That is one reason why we have a reporter here so that there will be no question about what I say to you and what you say to me. This record is for your protection, as much as for anybody else. You don't have to say anything to me, if you don't want to. However, you have already told us what happened, so there won't be any mistake about that," he said, leaning back in his chair and directing his full attention to the man who sat before him.

"I would like to. I really wish I could, but my attorney—"

"You don't have to have an attorney present to tell the truth, do you?" Neblett interrupted quickly.

"I know it. I've got the truth, but I can't say anything else."

Neblett paused a few moments before continuing. "Okay, Mr. Keys. Now let me ask you this. You spent Monday night at the ranch house—that is, the night before the shooting?"

"Yes, I was at home."

"Your wife and family were in Los Angeles?"

"Yes. They have been in Alhambra all winter."

"Then there was nobody there at the ranch with you?"

"That's right. Nobody else has been there all winter."

"And you have been looking after the place all winter in the absence of your family?"

"Yes, sir. That's right."

The D.A. quickly made a few notations on the pad in front of him, then continued. "Now, Mr. Keys. You have some stock that you graze out in that section?"

"Yes, I have cattle and I had Steve Kitchen, an Indian, up there two or three days riding with me."

"He wasn't there Tuesday?"

"No, not at that time, but he was before that."

"This morning you went out to your well over by the mill, didn't you?"

"Yes."

"And about what time was that?"

"As I said before, I didn't have a watch. I didn't fix any time, but I got up at the usual time, which is not very early."

"Out in the desert, what time do you consider early?"

Bill changed his position in the stiff-backed chair, then said, "Well, my usual time for getting up and getting ready to go out is around nine or ten o'clock. I never get away from home before that," he pointed out. "I have chores to do. I water the garden and trees first, and I have stock there sometimes too. When I get through, it is sometimes late."

The young District Attorney skillfully led Bill through the events of the shooting. As the questioning progressed, any

41

hesitation or anxiety that Bill might have had earlier about speaking without his attorney present disappeared, and he readily answered all of the questions that were put to him.

"Now, Mr. Keys, do you know where the bullet went that Bagley fired?"

"Well, I think it went close to me—right past my ear."

"Did it hit your car?"

"I don't know. There was perhaps two feet between me and the car. I was standing on the outside of the running board," Bill was careful to add.

"That was on the lefthand side of the car?"

"Yes, sir."

"And you had gotten out of your car on that side?"

"Yes."

"Then, Mr. Keys, you got your rifle out on that side also?"

"Yes, that's right."

"Had you shut the door when you first got out?"

"No. It was standing open, and the rifle was lying across the front seat."

Neblett made a few more quick notes. After a few moments' thought, he looked up once again. "All right. Now, when you got your rifle out, you stood by your car, but shut the door before you fired?"

"I shoved the door when I took my rifle out. The door usually closes anyway, because it's heavy. But I shut it, because I wanted to save the hinges."

"Fine. Now, Mr. Keys, after he fired at you and you shot back, were you still standing beside your car?"

"Yes. I stood beside the car and fired until he fell."

"You mean you didn't get behind that Joshua tree?"

"No. I stood in plain sight. Where I first took out the gun—that's where I stood," he said proudly.

"Which side of the road was Bagley on?"

"In the middle."

"The treads were on each side of him?"

"Yes."

"And where was that with relation to where Bagley finally dropped?"

"Well, he dropped ten or fifteen feet back of that towards the log and off to the left."

The District Attorney attempted to visualize Bill's testimony from his own personal knowledge of the shooting terrain.

"He fired, then you fired and hit him?"

"I must have creased him. I aimed to shoot the gun out of his hand."

"Now, when you hit him, he stepped out of the road?"

"Yes—over to the west side, but I kept on shooting while he was traveling. He had no chance to shoot after I began firing, because I had an automatic rifle."

"About how much time elapsed between his shot and your first shot?"

"Well, not very much—almost immediately."

"In other words, Mr. Keys, he shot, and you just started shooting?"

"You bet your life!" Bill said forcefully. "I wanted him to fire the first shot, because I thought he might speak to me— but he didn't. I didn't even raise my gun until he raised his and fired. I got it level, but I didn't sight."

"Then he hadn't much more than fired when you fired your three shots?"

"Yes, you bet your life! There was no possible chance for him to fire after I started shooting. My first shot creased his right arm, but my second shot must have hit his left arm and turned him completely around back toward the road."

"He was facing you due north at first?"

"That's right. Then he turned and pulled back towards the road and was standing until I fired the third shot."

Most of the D.A.'s remaining questions led Bill through the return trip to his ranch, his two hours of pumping water back at his well, and concluded with his drive down to Twentynine Palms to surrender to Dave Poste.

During the entire proceedings, Seymer Cash had silently transcribed all that had been said. He had barely looked up from his writing pad, which now was almost completely filled. Just when he thought that the questioning for the

43

morning was over, Bill was asked about his trips to the Bagley ranch house.

"Mr. Keys, was this week the only time you had been there?"

"No, sir. Three years before that I went to Bagley's house with some government surveyors."

"You say that was three years ago?"

"Yes, I wasn't there on my own. I was working for the government then. Bagley made nasty remarks at me and probably would have shot me there, if it hadn't been for the other men with me. But that time I never said a word to him. I guess that's the reason he didn't get enraged anymore than he was."

Neblett took in Keys' last remarks with silent interest. Then without hesitation he said, "Thank you, Mr. Keys. Everything you have told me today is true of your own knowledge?"

"Yes, that's the God's honest truth," Bill swore.

"And you made this statement freely and voluntarily?"

"Yes, sir."

"Thank you, Mr. Keys. The deputy will now take you back to your cell."

The lawman who had brought Bill there earlier had been standing silently in the rear of the room. He now moved forward to escort his prisoner from the office.

V

May 15, 1943
Saturday

Even though it was Saturday, the District Attorney, accompanied by Albert Kelly and Ray Pinker of the Los Angeles Police Department, drove out to Twentynine Palms on a special mission. Pinker was a forensic chemist, an expert at searching for physical evidence at the scene of a crime. His skills had been sharpened from over fourteen years of service with Los Angeles County.

The trio went directly to the 29 Palms Garage. There they were directed by its owner, Tom Martin, to the vehicle they had come to examine—Bill Keys' Victory Dodge with California license plates 6A2029.

The two lawmen stood outside talking briefly with Martin while Pinker checked the car thoroughly inside and out. He was looking for bloodstains. Finding none, he searched for possible bullet marks. A dent that resembled a ricochet mark on the edge of the door on the driver's side caught his attention. Closer examination convinced him that it had been caused by a small object of appreciable velocity striking the edge of the door, bending the metal and chipping the paint. With a small hand lens from his pocket, he studied the mark closer. In it he found debris that looked like lead. This he scraped off and put into an envelope for later laboratory analysis.

Pinker walked outside to discuss his findings with his two companions. The trio then left the garage and drove out of town into the National Monument, arriving at Bagley's ranch some forty minutes later. Here they parked on the dirt road south of the shooting site. Pinker searched for possible blood stains on the ground and on the brush near where the body had been found.

It wasn't long until he had discovered one large stain on the ground caked with sand. Another stain was located where Bagley's head had fallen, while others were found on the brush near where his feet had been. Blood samples were put into envelopes and marked with their locations for further lab study.

The group's last stop that afternoon was at Bill Keys' Desert Queen Ranch. Entering the house, they found a pair of work trousers, a belt still through its loops, draped over an overstuffed chair in the living room. Under close scrutiny, Pinker discovered what appeared to be blood stains on both legs. Taking the pants with him, he and the others returned to their car, departed the desert area and returned to Riverside.

VI

May 17, 1943
Monday

The Wiefels and Son hearse turned off Sepulveda Boulevard and passed through the west gates of the Sawtelle Veterans' Cemetery in West Los Angeles. Here it was joined by a military vehicle carrying a chaplain and honor guard. The two-car procession continued on, making a right turn onto Chateau Thierry Avenue, then proceeded the half mile to its end. There, with brief military services, former U.S. Navy Pharmacist's Mate First Class, Worth Webster Bagley was buried in Section 165 at 4:00 P.M.

VII

May 18, 1943
Tuesday

He had been awake for quite some time, silently staring up at the ceiling above the small metal frame bunk that was now his bed. Faraway thoughts slipped through his mind as he remembered the unbelievable events which had caused such a radical change in his life. He also worried about the fate of his cattle, now wandering unattended on Monument land, and hoped that his tanks were still providing water for them. In the back of his mind he realized that these same cattle would most likely have to be sold in order to help with his legal expenses. Perhaps Frances had been able to get one of her brothers or someone else to stay at their place until this mess could be cleared up, and he could get back to take charge of his life once more. There was so much work to be done—the garden had to be planted, the orchard watered, his fences mended and firewood cut for kitchen use. These, plus many other chores, are routine but necessary to keep a desert ranch alive.

Bill's thoughts had slipped back into the present, when he heard a jailer's voice announcing that it was time to get up. With that, he climbed off his bunk to begin another day of waiting. For an active man who had spent almost his entire life busily at work outdoors, the confinement of the small cell at the Riverside jail was especially hard. To keep his body in shape, he had begun exercising each morning after rising and again each night. Pushups and situps not only replenished his body strength and kept his muscles toned, but also helped to momentarily relax his mind from the strain of confinement.

After he had finished with his breakfast tray, he returned to sit on his bunk and to wait. He expected another visit that morning from his attorney, Paul D'Orr, to go over once again the events of the shooting. These two- and three-hour sessions were laying the groundwork for his defense.

Minutes slipped into hours. His solitude was finally interrupted by the sound of footsteps. He looked up as a jailer turned the key in the lock of his cell. The door opened and Frances and their friend Daisy Kiler entered. Since Frances did not drive, Daisy had brought her from Alhambra to see Bill. She and her husband, Warren, the Assistant Postmaster of Ontario, had known the Keys since the days before their marriage. Their close friendship had spanned the years.

Bill greeted the two women warmly. He had certainly missed Frances and their children at the ranch this past winter. They had decided that she should move to the Los Angeles area and rent a house there while the two youngest children, Pat and Phyllis, entered high school. Willis and Virginia, their two oldest, were already working there and had joined the rest of the family upon their arrival there last September.

Many of Bill and Frances' friends thought they were such an unlikely couple. He was an outdoors man, accustomed to rough work and hard times. Frances was a lady from the city whom Bill met, courted, married, and brought to the desert to be introduced to the rigors of his life there. But this small lady was made of tougher stock than many of her friends or family realized. She quickly adapted to her new life. Not even financial hard times nor the deaths of two babies and an eleven-year-old son could cause her to quit the desert that she had grown to love as much as her husband did. She kept her sorrows and disappointments to herself. Daisy always said her friend Frances was "a real brick" because of her seemingly endless strength and courage. She had worked long and hard beside Bill, giving him support through some of their worst times. As a result, their twenty-five-year marriage was solid. Therefore it wasn't surprising that she was here today, still supporting him in his greatest hour of need.

The two women brought Bill up to date on the ranch and the children. They helped to raise his spirits and left him with encouraging words.

Late that afternoon Bill was taken to Captain Walwrath's office for another interview, which began as soon as Bill was seated. Walwrath started his questions by asking Bill point blank, "Did you injure yourself the day of the shooting, or anytime before, Mr. Keys?"

"No, I didn't."

"Could you have that day or anytime shortly before, got any blood on your clothes?"

Bill thought for a moment before answering. "Well, I recently castrated a bull and might have then, but that was a couple of days before the shooting."

"All right, Mr. Keys, is there any possibility that the clothes you gave us the other day were not the ones you wore on the day of the shooting?"

Again, Bill thought for a few moments before answering.

"I'm not sure. I've got several old pairs of overalls. I could have worn any one of them. I've also got a pair of khaki pants that I could have been wearing."

The men then talked of other things. Bill spoke of his cattle and the trouble that he would have getting them rounded up during his detention. Walwrath listened without speaking, then when his prisoner had finished, he directed their conversation back to a subject that needed clarification.

"Mr. Keys, could you see Bagley's water truck from where the shooting took place?"

"No, not from there. The land's too low."

"When you were back at your mill, could you see Mrs. Bagley at the tank?"

"No, I didn't see her. It would be impossible unless she was walking around. It's just too far. But after I came back the second time, I walked up the road toward the south to

49

see if she was walking up toward me. I thought she might have heard the shooting."

"Well, was she?"

"No, I didn't see anybody."

That concluded the lawman's questions, and Bill Keys was taken back to his cell to wait once again.

The
Trial

VIII

July 7, 1943
Wednesday

Local newspapers predicted that it would be the longest trial to come before the Riverside courts since the Norcott murder case of 1929. Earlier that morning spectators who had filled the seats in the back of the courtroom listened as Prosecuting Attorney John Neblett questioned the prospective jurors. They had all been asked if their private affairs were in order so that they could remain in the event that the trial lasted three weeks.

Throughout this entire selection process, Bill Keys had sat quietly in the front of the room with his attorneys, Paul D'Orr and Thomas Reynolds. Behind him amongst the spectators sat Frances and a number of their friends. Bill was glad that his trial was finally about to begin. The seven weeks since the shooting had seemed like forever, and his concern for his cattle had grown with each day of his confinement.

During May and June, temperatures had climbed into the nineties and not a trace of rain had fallen on the Desert Queen Ranch. Finally, he had been granted permission to return to his home in the desert, accompanied by several deputies, so that he might pump water for his cattle. After this brief trip, his spirits lifted, and he had felt better. Since then, his son, Willis, and his brother-in-law, Buster, had returned at different times to care for the cattle. Otherwise, his animals would have perished.

It was almost 3:00 P.M. when all of the preliminaries

had been completed. Then the sound of Judge George R. Freeman's gavel echoed throughout the room of the Riverside Superior Court. With its fall case number 36496, the People of the State of California versus William F. Keys began.

The white-haired judge, a veteran of this court since his appointment in 1921, listened as John Neblett began the prosecution's case by calling Amos Brown as his first witness. The Deputy Surveyor was asked to familiarize everyone in the room with the general topography of the desert area where the shooting had taken place. Under cross examination by Paul D'Orr, special effort was made to point out all the roads, wells, structures, property lines, and other landmarks considered important. These were located on the map prepared by Brown, which was admitted as evidence. When his testimony concluded at 4:30, court adjourned to reconvene at 10:00 the following morning.

IX

July 8, 1943
Thursday

Four witnesses would be called to testify on the second day of the trial. Magistrate Dave Poste spoke in great detail of Bill Keys' confession at his office and of their trip to the Bagley ranch late on the afternoon of May 11th. Deputy Sheriff Meese followed, identifying photographs he had taken at the shooting site, while Dr. Leonard testified about his examination of Bagley's body. After he had described the wounds, the District Attorney questioned him concerning Bagley's colt revolver.

"Doctor, did you form an opinion as to the ability of the deceased to hold and cock a revolver after being wounded in the side?"

"Yes, sir. I did. My opinion was that the shock of the wound would have caused him to have dropped the revolver from his hand."

"How long, in your opinion, did the deceased survive such a wound?"

"I think that death was practically instantaneous," came his immediate answer.

After Dr. Leonard was excused, Jack Cones recounted his trip with Bill Keys and the other four men to the shooting site. Later in his testimony, District Attorney Neblett asked him to recall a conversation that he had had with Mr. Keys at Frank Bagley's service station in Twentynine Palms some three months previous.

"In the conversation that I had with Mr. Keys, he asked

me what he could do to get rid of that fellow, Worth Bagley, up there. I asked him what his reason was for wanting to get rid of him; wasn't he a property owner too? Well, he said that Bagley wouldn't let him use the road that crossed his— Bagley's property—that he had put glass in it, barricaded it, and had refused to let him across there to get to his own property which was located further up in the canyon from Bagley's well."

"Was anything further said?"

"I told Mr. Keys that the best thing he could do about it would be to take it to the court and to get a restraining order, or to have the court issue an order that he was to use the road. Mr. Keys said that they would not do anything about it. So I told him that was all that could be done. Then, just as I started to leave, Mr. Keys said, "Well, I'll just have to shoot him.""

"That's a lie," said Bill quietly, leaning over towards his attorneys. No one else heard his pronouncement, as Neblett turned his witness over to the defense attorneys for cross-examination.

Paul D'Orr began his questioning of Cones concerning his trips to and from the Bagley ranch, but because the time was late, Judge Freeman adjourned the court until the next morning. Bill Keys was returned to his cell where he thought about the day's testimony and wondered why Jack Cones had lied about him in court.

X

July 9, 1943
Friday

When Jack Cones returned to the witness stand the next morning, Paul D'Orr was ready for him. After hearing his testimony the previous day, he had decided that the character of Worth Bagley had to be revealed to the jury as soon as possible. Since it was impossible to put the deceased on the witness stand, he spent much of the night planning his necessary strategy.

"Mr. Cones, you knew Worth Bagley?"

"Yes, sir. I have talked with him on several occasions."

"You knew that he was a retired deputy sheriff from Los Angeles County, did you not?"

"Yes, sir. I understood that."

"And did he ever discuss with you the circumstances of his retirement?"

"Yes, sir. He stated to me that he had come out on sick leave several years before—I think in 1936."

"And in any of those conversations, did he tell you that he had been in the Riverside County Hospital?"

"No, he did not."

"Did he discuss with you any of his domestic difficulties?"

"I object to that as incompetent, irrelevant, and immaterial, and not proper cross-examination," exclaimed District Attorney Neblett, leaping to his feet before the constable could answer. "If the court pleases. Nothing was brought out from this witness regarding any conversation with the deceased relative to the circumstances under which he happened to be upon the desert or about his domestic affairs; and with respect to his domestic affairs, that is something that is entirely irrelevant in this case. It does not tend to prove or disprove any of the issues that we are concerned with here and is entirely out of order."

Paul D'Orr listened to the District Attorney's argument, then spoke to the judge.

"If the court please, this witness has made statements in this case to which I shall not refer. But I am entitled to search his motives fully to determine his relation with the dead man and his relations with and to the defendant. Any matter which may throw a light on those subjects, showing the intimacy of this witness with the deceased, is proper cross-examination."

Judge Freeman looked down at the two legal opponents and thought a few moments before making his ruling. Hardly a sound could be heard in the room, as he spoke.

"Mr. D'Orr, that may be true and your opinion of the rule is probably correct, but the question is whether or not it would be relevant. You cannot go into the details on outside matters, as it has nothing to do with the offense itself. I will therefore sustain the objection."

"Then your Honor sustains the objection on the question of discussing his domestic affairs?" Paul D'Orr asked.

"Yes," came Judge Freeman's reply.

With this setback, the defense attorney carefully framed his next question.

"Did he ever tell you that his wife had sued him for divorce on the grounds that he had threatened the lives of his neighbors, including the defendant, William F. Keys?"

"I object again, your Honor," exclaimed Neblett. "If the court please, the question, in my opinion, is highly prejudicial and irrelevant."

"Your Honor," contradicted the defense attorney, "counsel mistakes my purpose. The question directed to this witness was with the design of showing that the deceased was a dangerous, erratic, and threatening character. I can prove that by statements of the deceased to a witness without violating the rule of hearsay."

Judge Freeman was quick to interrupt the legal argument that was imminent. "I think that we had probably better settle this now." He turned to face the jury. "You may retire, but I will admonish the jury not to converse among yourselves while you are out of this room."

After the twelve men and women had filed out, he turned to the court reporter. "Please read the last question again."

The court reporter looked at his notes, then read, "The defense attorney asked, 'Did he ever tell you that his wife had sued him for divorce on the grounds that he had threatened the lives of his neighbors, including the defendant, William F. Keys?'"

The judge then sat back to listen to the lengthy arguments that the two legal counsels would present to justify their positions concerning the legality of allowing testimony concerning Worth Bagley's character. After hearing both counsels, he once again sustained Neblett's objection and had the jury recalled.

Paul D'Orr withdrew his question and the trial resumed. "Now, Mr. Cones, don't answer this next question until counsel has had an opportunity to object," he cautioned. "He may or may not wish to do so. Did the deceased, in any of these conversations with you in Twentynine Palms, tell you that he had or that his condition had been diagnosed as one of hysteria and mental disturbance, by any psychiatrists or physicians in Los Angeles County or at Sawtelle or at the Riverside County Hospital?"

"I object. It's hearsay, incompetent, irrelevant, and immaterial," voiced John Neblett.

"Objection sustained," came the official word from the judge.

"Mr. Cones, you said that Mr. Bagley talked with you in Twentynine Palms on one or more occasions. Did he ever complain to you about Mr. Keys?"

"No, sir. He did not."

"When Mr. Keys came to see you about three months previous to the May eleventh incident, did he mention how long the road in question had been used by the public?"

"I hardly think so, because at the time, I didn't know what

he was referring to."

"Did he tell you that the road was used by the public before the Southern Pacific Railroad even patented the land which was later sold to Mr. Bagley?"

"Yes."

"Did he tell you that before that land was patented, when the desert was free, that this well, now known as the Bagley well, was called the Desert Queen well, and that it was drilled by, and used by, a man named Morgan, and that it was used by Mr. Keys for many years in connection with his Desert Queen Mine?"

The constable answered quickly, "Well, he told me that it was the old Desert Queen well, but he didn't tell me anything about who it was used by."

"Now Mr. Cones, did he tell you that when it was wild government land, and before it had been patented, that he removed the windmill from this well which he had bought from Mr. Morgan and moved it to his ranch? Did he tell you that?" D'Orr asked, looking straight at Cones.

"Well, he mentioned the windmill."

"He did tell you, didn't he, that Mr. Bagley had come to him years later when he bought this place from the Southern Pacific Railroad and demanded that he bring that windmill back?"

"The statement he made to me was that that was his well, that he had a windmill on it, and that he had been given permission to remove the windmill from that well. He did not tell me who it was that drilled it or anything of that nature."

"And in this same conversation with Mr. Keys, did he tell you anything about Bagley's complaint that he moved his little herd of sixty or seventy-five head of cattle along this road twice a year from Queen Valley into Pleasant Valley, and Pleasant Valley back into Queen Valley? Did he tell you that, Mr. Cones?"

"No, he never did mention anything to me about a disagreement concerning his cattle, only that he had to go over that road to pump water for his cattle."

"Did Mr. Keys tell you that after a conversation with

Bagley concerning his cattle traveling over this public road, that he had agreed to build, and did in fact build, a barbed-wire fence at his own expense around about eighty acres of Mr. Bagley's land—including his house?"

"Do you mean our conversation at the service station?"

"Yes, I do," said the defense attorney.

Cones thought a few moments before answering. "Well, he didn't there, but he did later when we were waiting for the other deputies on the day of the shooting. He said something about having five men build a fence, and one thing or another on Bagley's property."

"Now, Mr. Cones, when you were out there, you saw that fence which makes a great semi-circle with the rocky shelves and cliffs, and encloses about eighty acres of Bagley's land around his house, didn't you?"

"Well, I could see the fence some distance on each side of the stock gate, as you cross over to the well."

"Is that the fence that Mr. Keys pointed out to you as having been built by him?"

"Why, he just said that he built a fence there."

"Now, did he tell you that Bagley had agreed that he would build that fence so the cattle couldn't come anywhere around his place, and that he had no objection to his using the road? Think hard before you answer!"

Again, the room was perfectly still as everyone's attention was keenly focused on the witness and his pending reply to the question. Then Cones spoke.

"I think Bagley agreed to his building the fence."

"Did Mr. Keys tell you that after he got that fence built, that Bagley then told him to keep off of the place?"

"No, I don't recollect him ever saying that he was told to stay off of there."

"Are you sure?" D'Orr asked again, looking straight at the witness.

"Yes!" came Cones' firm answer.

D'Orr waited a moment before posing his next question.

"Did Mr. Keys tell you—that was the time when he came down and talked to you and asked you what could be done with Mr. Bagley—that Bagley had shot some of his cattle

61

in the belly with a .22 rifle and that they had soon sickened and died?"

"No, he didn't mention anything about that then. He just wanted to know what could be done to get rid of Bagley."

"You mean he didn't tell you about some previous difficulty that he had had with Mr. Bagley over his cattle?"

"Not at that time."

"All right then, at some later time?" D'Orr asked, raising his voice momentarily.

"Yes, when we were driving over from the Bagley ranch to wait for the County Sheriff's deputies and the coroner."

"Let's leave that out for now and go on with your conversation at the service station. Now Mr. Keys asked your advice about what could be done about Mr. Bagley. Did you understand that he was consulting you as a peace officer?"

"Yes."

"And you say that you told him to resort to the courts to get an injunction?" the defense challenged.

"That's right. It was my honest opinion that it should have been taken to the courts."

"Now Mr. Cones, you would expect a man who wanted to keep the peace and avoid violence to ask the advice of a law enforcement officer, would you not?"

"Well, I would expect him to go to the District Attorney whose business it is. That was the reason why our conversation did not last any longer than it did."

"Did you also tell Mr. Keys to keep out of that territory and go all around to his property?"

"I did. It was none of my business whether he went all the way around or not. I did say that I would go a long ways before I would have any trouble with anybody," concluded the constable.

"Thank you, Mr. Cones. I have no more questions."

"Neither does the prosecution," added John Neblett. "You may be excused."

As Jack Cones was leaving the witness stand, the District Attorney called Walter Ketchum of the National Park Service to testify. He stated that he was present when Bill Keys was taken back to the Bagley property by Constable

62

Cones. The ranger further stated that the defendant had made no direct statements to him, and after a very few minutes of questioning, he was excused.

When Duane Jacobs testified, he recounted his meeting with the defendant and Constable Cones on the main Monument road in Queen Valley. His testimony concentrated on their conversation then, as well as the one which he had witnessed at the site of the shooting. Then John Neblett asked the Acting Custodian of the National Monument about a previous meeting with Bill Keys.

"How long have you know the defendant, Mr. Keys?"

"About seven months."

"Had you ever had any conversations with him prior to May 11, 1943 regarding this road?"

"At one time, I did."

"And do you recall when that was?"

"It was in January of last winter. I had gone into Mr. Keys' ranch to discuss some things with him, and he mentioned this problem."

"Was anyone else present?"

"Yes. Besides Mr. Keys, one of our Park Service road men was with me."

"And does the Bagley ranch lie within the boundaries of Joshua Tree National Monument?"

"Yes, sir. It does."

"What conversation did you have with Mr. Keys at that time, relative to the road?"

"Well, Mr. Keys told me that there was a road going over to his well, and that Bagley would not let him use it. He asked me what he should do to use this road. I told him that it was out of our jurisdiction, because it was private land. So we really didn't have anything to do with it, and that was all that was said about it."

"All right, Mr. Jacobs. Now when you were at the scene of the shooting on May 11th, was anything said by the defendant in your presence with respect to a section marker?"

"Yes, sir. He told the officers from San Bernardino about the county line, but none of us knew where the line was. Then Mr. Keys said, 'There's a corner stake right over the hill,' and pointed immediately east of our location at the Joshua tree. Later on, I did walk over the hill and find the stake. I hadn't known that it was there either."

"Was there any vegetation covering this stake?"

"No. You could see it easily."

"Your witness, Mr. D'Orr."

As the District Attorney returned to his seat, the defense attorney hurriedly glanced down at his notes momentarily, then approached Duane Jacobs on the witness stand.

"Was there formerly a man connected with the Monument by the name of Jim Cole?"

"Yes. He's a lieutenant in the army now. He left us on the 31st of October last year."

"Did Mr. Keys tell you at the time of your conversation at his ranch, that he had previously talked to Mr. Cole about the road matter?"

"He may have, but I can't recall it."

"Do you remember his telling you that Mr. Cole said to him that the road had been used for years and years, and so far as he knew, Mr. Keys had a right to use it?"

"No, sir. I don't remember that."

D'Orr paused for a moment, framing his next question, then asked Jacobs, "So there won't be any confusion in anyone's mind, you might explain to these ladies and gentlemen the difference between a Monument and a Park."

"Well, Joshua Tree isn't a Park. It's a Monument. While both areas are administered by the National Park Service, a National Monument is created by Presidential proclamation, and a National Park is created only by an Act of Congress. A National Monument is usually an area of lesser importance than a National Park. Both areas are set aside to preserve some scenic natural wilderness or attractive recreational area for the use of the people."

"How much area, Mr. Jacobs, in square miles, does this Joshua Tree National Monument cover?"

"About 838,000 acres, which is twelve hundred and some square miles."

"And in your capacity as Acting Custodian of this

National Monument, have you driven over a good deal of that territory?"

"A good deal of it yes, but there are lots of roads that I haven't been over yet. There's a mass of trails—old miners' trails. You can drive almost any place just by wandering around."

"And these roads have been there since time immemorial, Mr. Jacobs?"

"Yes. More or less."

"Thank you, Mr. Jacobs. That's all."

As Duane Jacobs was stepping down to resume his seat in the courtroom, Judge Freeman spoke. "Counsels, I think it's time for a short recess. The jury is admonished as before."

Many of those seated in the rear of the room rose immediately and exited into the hallway. Frances Keys came forward to where her husband was still seated with his attorneys. With her were old friends, Lee and Chet Perkins. Before their marriage, Lee had been one of a succession of teachers who had taught the Keys children at their Desert Queen Ranch. The trio greeted Bill, then talked quietly amongst themselves through the rest of the fifteen minute recess.

When court resumed, Perry H. Green was called as the next witness for the prosecution. After preliminary questioning, John Neblett narrowed the scope of his inquiry.

"Did you go to the Bagley ranch on the afternoon of May 11, 1943?"

"Yes, sir."

"And with whom did you go?"

"Mr. Heap and Mr. Russell, deputies from our office."

"And upon your arrival at the scene of the shooting, did you discuss or observe any signs with respect to the body of the deceased?"

"Yes, sir. I saw one sign about one hundred feet south of the body by the side of a Joshua tree."

"Did you pick up anything at that point?"

"Yes, a hammer."

"And did you observe any obstruction in the road in the vicinity of the spot where you picked up the hammer and the sign?"

"Yes. There was a dead Joshua tree lying across the road—oh, probably forty or fifty feet from where I picked up the sign and hammer."

"Did you see any other signs in the immediate vicinity of the spot?"

"Yes, sir, on the north of the body in the middle of the road."

"By the 'road' do you refer to the road which ran alongside of the point where the body lay?"

"Yes, sir."

"Now, Mr. Green, I have two photographs here which I'd like you to identify for the court," he said, handing them to the lawman.

Green looked briefly at each before speaking. "This one is of the road near where the body was found." Then he held the other one toward the District Attorney. "This one here is the dead Joshua tree of which I just spoke."

After identifying the hammer and warning signs, he was excused.

Deputy Harry Heap's testimony concentrated on his trip to the Bagley ranch, on his stopping to examine the glass in the road, and of having seen the hammer and signs. Then he was asked by the District Attorney, "Did you notice anything unusual about Mr. Bagley's body?"

"Well, I paid particular attention to the position of the gun in his hand. The three fingers were wrapped around the butt with the forefinger extended," he answered.

"As indicated in this photograph which the court has marked as Exhibit F-1?" questioned Neblett, as he handed it to his witness.

"Yes, that's right," he answered, after looking at it. "The ground underneath the arm, including the elbow, was loose sand. The elbow had made a deep indentation in the ground—I would say, up at least an inch on the arm. As far as I could tell, I couldn't see where there were any drag marks of the arm showing where it moved a particle. The end of the barrel was very near to the ground. You could see in the soft sand that the barrel had never even touched the ground."

"You observed no indentations in the ground?" Neblett said, emphasizing the point for the jury's attention.

"No. There were none at the end of the barrel."

"Now, Mr. Heap. Could you please describe the wounds that you observed on the deceased?"

"Well, the left arm was almost shot off. It was in a mutilated condition."

"And did you observe any other wounds?"

"Not until the body was moved. Then I saw where the bullet had evidently entered the body. I also felt what I thought was the bullet in his right side just under the skin."

The District Attorney continued his questioning, asking him about the footprints near the body, the barricades, and the various conversations which he had had with the defendant on the day of the shooting, until court adjourned late that afternoon.

XI

July 13, 1943
Tuesday

When court reconvened on the fourth day, Bill Keys, his attorneys and the others in the courtroom watched as Deputy Sheriff William T. Russell was called to the stand. After being sworn in, District Attorney Neblett's questions skillfully led his witness through his trip to the Bagley ranch, his meeting of Constable Cones, and the ride to the shooting scene in Cones' car. In the course of his testimony he related several of the conversations that he had held with Bill Keys that day.

"Mr. Witness, you accused Mr. Keys of having shot the decedent the night before?"

"No, I didn't accuse him of it. I asked him if he hadn't shot—I mean, if this shooting hadn't occurred the night before?"

"Had you seen Dr. Leonard at the scene before you had this conversation with Mr. Keys?"

"No, sir."

"You had no statement from any person, any medical man, or otherwise at that time, as to how long it had been since death occurred?"

"No, sir."

"Well, was that question impelled by any evidence brought to you, either through your own senses or from any other person, that the body had been in that position all night?"

"I would say through my own senses."

"Your witness," said John Neblett, walking in front of the

stand and returning to his seat at the table directly opposite the one where Bill Keys and his attorneys sat.

In beginning his cross-examination, Paul D'Orr concentrated on Russell's immediate testimony.

"Mr. Russell, if I understand you correctly, you suggested to Mr. Keys that he shot the deceased the night before?"

"No, sir. I did not suggest it," replied the deputy cautiously.

"Well, you said you accused him of it, didn't you?"

"I didn't say I accused him of it. I asked him if this shooting could not have happened the night before—or did not happen the night before."

"You also accused him, did you not, of having shot the deceased and then put the gun in his hand?"

"No, I don't think I accused him of that."

"You say you don't think so? Did you accuse him of something similar?"

"I did not accuse Mr. Keys of the crime," Russell stated confidently.

"Did you tell him that he shot this man to death, and then put the gun in his hand?"

"No. I told him from the evidence that it looked to me as though the gun was put in his hand after the man was shot. It also looked to me as though the man was shot while he was on the ground. I asked him if he did not shoot from his automobile."

"Is that what you told Mr. Keys?" D'Orr said, raising his voice, as if questioning the veracity of this witness.

"I asked him that."

"You say you asked him that? You told him that it also looked to you that he was shot from the ground, and that somebody put the gun in his hand?"

"No, I don't know that I asked Mr. Keys that. I only expressed that as my opinion."

"Then I asked you, if you did not suggest to Mr. Keys, or accuse Mr. Keys, take it either way you want, of having put the gun in the deceased's hand. You told me that you did," he said, continuing to raise his voice.

"I object, your Honor. That is argumentative and calls for

a conclusion on the part of the witness," voiced the District Attorney. "He stated what he said. If he suggests and that is an accusation, then that is a conclusion for the jury to draw."

The defense attorney was not taken back by this objection.

"Your Honor. That is a proper method of cross-examination."

"Will the court reporter read back the last question?" Judge Freeman asked.

The question was read, and after a moment's contemplation, the judge overruled the District Attorney's objection. Paul D'Orr continued with his cross-examination.

"Then if you did not suggest that, or ask Mr. Keys that question, did you express your opinion aloud in Mr. Keys' presence?"

"I may have expressed that. Yes, sir. And Mr. Keys may have heard it."

"Did you say that directly to Mr. Keys?"

"I did not."

"Did you say it in his presence?"

"Yes, he was there. Whether he heard me or not, I don't know."

"Now, Mr. Russell, Mr. Keys made the statement repeatedly to you and to those other officers that he had fired the shots which brought down the deceased. That is true, isn't it?"

"That is true."

"So you knew that the man who shot Worth Bagley was Mr. Keys?"

"Yes, sir."

"Had you made any examination of the body to determine which way the bullets ranged that struck the deceased in the side?"

"Not at the time. No, sir."

"Did you examine the right arm?"

"As much as I could from viewing it without moving the arm. I didn't touch the body."

"Did you examine the left arm?"

"I didn't examine the body outside of viewing it from what I could see without moving it."

"I see. Yet at that time you expressed the opinion to Mr. Keys that the man was shot on the ground?"

"It looked that way to me."

"Did you make that statement before the coroner came?"

"I did. I made that statement when I first viewed the body. I also made it after the coroner arrived when I told him what my opinion was."

"You told the coroner afterwards? Did you tell Mr. Keys your opinion after the coroner had arrived?"

"I did not."

"Let me ask you another question, Mr. Russell. Did you see the pistol that was in the hand of the deceased?"

"Yes, I did."

The defense attorney walked over to the exhibit table and picked up a pistol which had a white tag on it, and looked towards John Neblett.

"Counsel. Is this it?"

"Yes, Mr. D'Orr," came the D.A.'s reply.

D'Orr turned and walked back to the witness with the weapon. "Mr. Russell. Does this look like the pistol that you saw?" The witness glanced down at the weapon that the defense attorney held out toward him.

"Yes, it does."

"Will you please describe this pistol to the jury?"

"Yes. It's a Colt .38 calibre revolver, with target sights, and a .44 frame capable of holding six cartridges."

"And can that pistol be fired by double action? That is, by simply pulling the trigger, when the hammer is not cocked?"

"I would say that it can. Yes, sir."

"Can the hammer be cocked and the pistol then fired by pulling the trigger?"

"Yes, sir. It should be, unless it has been worked over to prevent it."

"Mr. Russell. Are you a pistol shot?"

"Not an expert. No, sir."

"Have you fired pistols of this type?"

"I have."

71

"And what type of pistol are you and the other deputies in your detail equipped?"

"There is no standard. Most of the boys carry Colts or .38 Smith and Wessons."

"I have no further questions for this witness."

"That is all then," added the District Attorney, and Deputy Russell left the stand.

The prosecution's next witness was Deputy Sheriff Charles B. Worchester, a veteran of thirty years service with Riverside County. He identified Bagley's pistol as the one that he had seen in the hand of the deceased at the scene of the shooting, and as the one that he had examined in his office for fingerprints. He further testified that he had found none on the gun during his examination. Since D'Orr chose not to cross-examine him, the witness was excused.

Like the witnesses before him, C. F. McCracken retold the story of the shooting that Bill Keys had related to him as well as to the other officers with him on the day of the shooting and on the following day. Using a large board covered with photographs of the shooting site, this plaintiff's witness was asked to mark with blue crayon the various places where Bill Keys and Bagley had been during the entire confrontation. He stated that at the time Bagley fired, he was only 104 feet south of Keys. He then marked Bagley's movements on the photograph.

"Bagley moved twenty-six feet west and south, then traveled seventeen feet west before falling. His body was 132 feet from the Joshua tree where Mr. Keys had stood during the entire time. These other photographs on the edge here," he said, pointly directly at them, "show Mr. Keys' car and the dent in its door."

In cross-examination, Paul D'Orr questioned him about his trip to the Bagley house. "Mr. McCracken, did you go over to the Bagley house while you were in that vicinity on the 11th or 12th?"

"Yes, I did—on the 12th."

"Did you find a sign over at Bagley's house which contained any printed or reading matter?"

"Yes, sir."

72

"And what did it say?"

"It was a sign on the northeast side of the house. I believe that it said, 'Warning. This property protected by gun traps,' or some such statement."

"Thank you. Your witness."

The District Attorney approached McCracken as D'Orr returned to his seat next to the defendant.

"The name 'Keys' did not appear on that sign, did it?"

"No, sir. It didn't."

"Had you seen other similar signs in that area, Mr. McCracken?"

"I have seen many of them in desert properties."

"Thank you, sir. Mr. D'Orr."

Once again the defense attorney returned to begin re-cross-examination of the witness.

"Mr. McCracken. Can you remember the location of any of these signs that you have seen on those desert properties?"

"I certainly can," the witness replied.

"When you saw these other signs about gun traps, what did you understand them to mean?"

"Well, I know what it means. It's a warning to any transient or anyone else that might be tempted to break into the property that they just hadn't better."

"Did you make any investigations at Bagley's house to find out whether he had any spring guns?"

"Yes, I saw some spring guns there."

John Neblett returned to clear up one more question concerning the spring guns.

"Did you see them set up, Mr. McCracken?"

"No, sir. I didn't."

"Thank you. That's all."

As McCracken left the stand, Captain W. W. Walwrath was the last witness of the day to be called on behalf of the plaintiff. In his testimony he described the trip with Mr. Keys to his ranch to gather his clothing. Later he told of the conversation that had taken place in his office with the defendant concerning the possible origins of the bloodstains on those clothes. After a few minutes of cross-examination, he was excused and court was adjourned for the day.

XII

July 14, 1943
Wednesday

When court reconvened for the fifth time, the prosecution's witness was Dr. Wayne K. Templeton of Riverside. After he was sworn in, John Neblett began his questioning.

"Dr. Templeton, please describe any wounds that you observed upon the body of the deceased at the time you made the autopsy on May 13th of this year."

"Certainly. There was a large wound in the inner surface of the left forearm. The muscles there were torn in fragments, both bones were shattered, and the wound was pretty well filled with dirt. There was also a slight abrasion on the right arm just above the elbow, and also, a wound slightly posterior to the axillary line on the left side about fifteen inches below shoulder level." Using the District Attorney as his model, he showed the location of each of the wounds, after which Neblett returned to his questioning.

"Doctor. From your examination of the wound on the right forearm, did you form any opinion as to the position of that arm at the time the deceased sustained that wound?"

"Yes, that the arm was probably down."

"Do you mean the upper portion of the arm was down—that is, from the elbow to the shoulder?"

"Yes, that is correct."

"And did you form any opinion, Doctor, as to whether or not a person, after sustaining such wound as you described, would be able to hold a gun in his right hand?"

"He would not hold it very long."

"Counsel, you may cross-examine."

Paul D'Orr approached the witness. "Doctor, a wound like that would cause a man to drop immediately to the ground, wouldn't it? A lethal wound of the kind that you have just described, entering the body of a man on the left side, as this wound was made, would kill him almost instantaneously?"

"That is correct."

"And he would, to use a common phrase, 'drop in his tracks'?"

"That's right."

"Is it possible that this lethal wound in his left side might have been caused by the same bullet which shattered the left arm?"

"It's very possible."

"From the evidence which you observed during the autopsy, would you say conclusively, that the bullet ranged upward after it entered the body of the deceased?"

"I would."

"And that the firearm from which the bullet was expelled, was in such a position, or else the body of the deceased was in such a position, that when the bullet entered the body, it would range upward?"

"The bullet might have been deflected somewhat from hitting something beforehand. That could be possible too."

"Yes, but not after it entered the body of the deceased?"

"No, not after it entered the body."

"Fine. Now let us assume for the moment that the ground on which the decedent stood at the time he received the lethal blow, was approximately four and a half feet higher than the ground on which the man who fired the shot stood. Let us also assume that both men were about the same height. If this is correct then can we assume that the bullet fired would enter the deceased in an upward path, as you have described?"

Dr. Templeton paused momentarily, then answered, "Yes, we can assume that."

"Now, Doctor, returning to the skin abrasion on the right

arm—the abrasion that you described is some distance from the ulnar nerve, isn't it?"

"That's perfectly correct."

"As a matter of fact, Doctor, it isn't near any nerve of consequence at all?"

"Again, that is perfectly correct."

"Thank you, sir. Mr. Neblett."

The District Attorney exchanged places with D'Orr. "Doctor, I don't believe I asked but what was, in your opinion, the cause of death?"

"Death was due to shock and to hemorrhage caused by a bullet wound in the abdomen, which passed through the left kidney, spleen, dorsal aorta, left diaphragm and right lung," came his confident, professional answer.

"Thank you, that is all. Mr. D'Orr, your witness."

Once again, as Paul D'Orr returned to the witness, his mind was racing through his next line of questioning. "Doctor. In examining the body of the deceased, did you have before you, any history of former wounds or other lesions of either arm?"

"Yes."

"What was that history?"

"Just a moment!" Neblett interrupted vehemently. "I object to that as incompetent, irrelevant and immaterial, and not proper cross-examination. Counsel's first question as to whether or not he had before him any such history would be proper. But as to what the nature of those other injuries was, I do not think it material, your Honor."

"Counsel is wrong about that!" countered D'Orr.

Judge Freeman took off his glasses, considering for the moment the legality of the objection. Then he said, "It depends upon what might develop. Overruled." D'Orr was smiling, as he returned to his next question.

"Now, Doctor—what did you observe?"

"There was some atrophy of the muscles in the left forearm and in the hand which was more marked in the fingers. In other words, the muscles were smaller in the left hand than in the right one."

"Did I understand you to say that the bullet when you

76

found it was just under the skin between the sixth and seventh ribs?"

"That's correct."

"Now, Doctor, if we use my assistant, Mr. Thomas Reynolds, seated over there next to the defendant, as a model, would you please show the jury where the bullet entered the body of the deceased?" D'Orr handed Templeton a colored pencil as they both stepped to where the young assistant was now standing. Here the doctor marked a spot on the white shirt for all to see. It was approximately fifteen inches down from the shoulder on the seam.

"Very good, Doctor. That's an easy way for us to make a demonstration—as long as my assistant doesn't mind," D'Orr said, smiling. Then he pointed to the area under Reynolds' armpit. "Let's assume that this seam, or little pleat, represents the axillary line. It extends from the center of the armpit down to the top or approximate top of the innominate bone. Now, if you would also indicate on this shirt the point beneath which you found the bullet."

Templeton made another mark.

"It's almost under the right nipple, isn't it?"

"Yes, sir," came the doctor's reply. "Just beneath it."

"All right. Thank you sir. Mr. Neblett."

Neblett got up, pushing his chair back, and walked around the table to the front of the courtroom.

"Now, Doctor. What would be the muscular reaction, as a result of sustaining this bullet wound that you have just described?"

"Well, immediately, there might be a little bit of muscle tightening, but they would relax just as quickly upon death."

"Then upon death, there is complete relaxation?" Neblett asked to re-emphasize the point for the jury's benefit.

"Yes, that's correct."

"That's all. Mr. D'Orr."

The defense attorney was still considering his opponent's last question and the witness's response, as he walked forward. Within a few moments, he was ready with his own strategy to counter the prosecution's point.

"Doctor, a sudden, lethal wound which produces shock,

or a non-lethal one which produces a profound shock, might cause a voluntary or involuntary contraction of the muscles momentarily?"

"That's correct."

"Now if death is practically instantaneous, then there immediately follows a relaxation of the muscles to a certain extent?"

"That's right."

"But a dead man won't stretch out his fingers, will he?"

"No, he will not."

"Very good. And finally when rigor mortis sets in, there's a hardening or stiffening of the tissues of the human body which leaves a man rigid or practically so?"

"That's right," replied the doctor.

"Thank you, sir. Your witness."

John Neblett continued the line of questioning started by Paul D'Orr. "Until rigor mortis sets in, the condition that you have described as relaxation is present, is it not?"

"That's right."

"There's no definite time when rigor mortis would so set in in a particular case, is there?"

"No. It's a gradual process."

"Rigor mortis may not exist for several hours?"

"Well, not too many hours. It's a gradual process and will probably start within a couple of hours."

"Mr. D'Orr, you may cross-examine."

The defense attorney was now sure of the direction that John Neblett was leading the witness. As he approached the stand, he knew that he had to show the jury another side to the evidence that was being presented.

"Doctor, when you speak of relaxation, if a man falls in his tracks in a given position, his members outstretched or crumpled, his hands either in a cramped or relaxed position, his limbs describing a certain pattern, relaxation will not produce changes in the position of his members or cause him to clutch his hand, if it was open, or open his hand if it was clutched?"

"Well, if his hand was clutched, relaxation might let it relax from that clutch."

"But would he spread his fingers out, Doctor?"

"No, sir. He wouldn't."

"Thank you. Mr. Neblett."

Now John Neblett knew that he had to get one last point for the benefit of his argument.

"Now, Doctor. With respect to this period of tension immediately after the condition of shock, will you describe that reaction or tension, as to how long it would continue?"

"You might immediately get a tightening. If the man dies a few seconds later, then it will go away almost immediately."

"Then upon death, that tension ceased?" Neblett asked pointedly.

"Yes, sir. That tension ceased," came the doctor's definite reply.

"That's all of the questions I have. Mr. D'Orr, do you have more questions of this witness?"

"No more questions. Thank you, Doctor."

After the lunch recess, Deputy Coroner Cash began his testimony, using his shorthand notes to recount conversations that Bill Keys had made—both at the scene of the shooting, and later in the District Attorney's office.

He was followed on the stand by Dr. Frank R. Webb, the Chief Autopsy Surgeon of Los Angeles, who would be the last witness called that day. Like Dr. Templeton had before him, he described the wounds that he had observed on Worth Bagley's body. The District Attorney's carefully framed questions were building a damaging case against the defendant.

"Doctor, did you form any opinion as to how long the deceased survived after he sustained the wound in his left side?"

"Well, basing my opinion upon my autopsy findings would indicate that there was a complete and immediate collapse after he received these wounds."

"Did the course of the bullet, as determined by you, approach the spine of the deceased?"

"It passed in front of the edge of the spine."

"What would be the effect of the bullet following the

course into the body of the deceased with respect to his nervous system?"

"It would have paralyzed the nervous system from concussion."

"What significance, if any, did the dirt or foreign matter that you found in the wound have in arriving at your conclusion?"

"Well, the dirt and foreign matter were imbedded into the flesh. If it had simply been spread over, I might have thought it was due to just the wind blowing the sand. As it was imbedded in that manner, I would infer that either the bullet had stirred up dust which was carried into the wound at the time of its impact, or that the arm had been dragged in the sand."

Neblett paused to let the jury ponder that information before he asked his next important question. "Did you form an opinion, Doctor, as to the ability of the deceased to hold a revolver in his right hand after sustaining the fatal wound on his left side?"

"Yes, I did. After sustaining the fatal wound, I would expect complete collapse. Had he been holding a gun at that time in an erect position, that gun would have naturally fallen from his hand."

"From your examination, did you form an opinion as to the position of the deceased at the time he sustained the fatal wound?"

"The only thing that I could infer from my examination is that the arm would have to be drawn upward and flexed, or after he was in a prone position, the hand would be placed downward, as if a person was supporting his side or crawling."

"What do you mean by a prone position, Doctor?"

"Lying with the face downward."

"Now, did you also form an opinion as to whether or not the wound that you observed in the left arm of the deceased, as well as the wound in his left side, were caused by one or more bullets?"

"It's my opinion that they were caused by one bullet."

The District Attorney paused once again. "And did you

80

form any opinion as a result of your examination, as to the position of the deceased with respect to the ground at the time that he sustained such a wound?"

"All that I could say was that the arm would have to be in that flexed position up near the body at the time the wound was received. It's rather an unusual position to assume with the arm and shoulder drawn up that way in an erect position. Now, if the person was lying on the ground, face downward, or partly on his abdomen, and his hand up to the side there, as if crawling, then that would be a very likely position with the course of the wound that I found," Doctor Templeton theorized.

"Did the presence of dirt and foreign matter in the wound affect your opinion in that respect?"

"Yes, sir. It did."

"In what respect?"

"In the fact that if the body was on the ground, the force of the bullet—that is, the air pressure of the bullet, would stir up sand and dirt as it entered the body."

"Thank you, Doctor. Your witness, Mr. D'Orr."

John Neblett smiled coyly at Paul D'Orr as they passed near the witness stand. His skillful questions had presented to the jury his theory of how the shooting of Worth Bagley actually took place. It would now be up to Paul D'Orr to try and disprove this theory, if Bill was to have any chance for acquittal.

"Doctor, how would the force of the bullet, the suction of the air, or the vacuum carry the sand and grit into the wound, if the bullet passed entirely through the arm including the bones and tissue before entering the side of the deceased?"

"Well, if it had passed directly through the arm forming a hole, I could expect to find that only at the entrance. But as it was, the whole front of the arm was torn open, due to the bullet's force and the effect of the fractured bones tearing their way out," the doctor answered confidently.

"And it's your opinion that one bullet caused the wound in the arm and the wound in the body?"

"It is."

"Does your opinion exclude every other possibility and hypothesis?"

"I try to exclude every other possibility and hypothesis when I draw my opinion."

"You did determine that the body had probably been exposed out there in the desert for about twelve hours?"

"I did. But now I don't think that it was quite as long as that. The deceased died somewhere between ten and eleven in the morning and the body was removed that evening."

"Did you make any inquiries or did you talk with any of the men who were assumed to have removed the body from the ranch and transported it to Banning?"

"The only person that I know of was Mr. Chapman, who was working at the funeral parlor."

"And did you talk with him, Doctor?"

"I certainly did at the time of the autopsy on May 13th."

"Do you recollect when he told you that it was removed?"

"I understood him to say about eleven o'clock was the time that he did the embalming, so it must have been an hour or so before that when the body was removed."

"Were you told how many men had been at the scene between 4:30 in the afternoon of May 11th and the time that the body was removed from the desert?"

"No, sir."

"Thank you, Doctor. That's all. Mr. Neblett."

As John Neblett returned to take his standing position in front of the witness stand, he said, "Yes, I only have one more question for this witness. Doctor, what in your opinion, would be the effect upon the ability of the deceased to hold a revolver in his right hand, assuming that he was standing erect, after sustaining the wound in his left side?"

"I would expect complete collapse and the dropping of the gun," came the answer that the District Attorney wanted everyone to hear.

"That's all. Thank you. Mr. D'Orr."

Again John Neblett felt that he had achieved another victory for the prosecution, as he returned to resume his seat. But Paul D'Orr was not a man to give up easily. He knew how to take some of the power out of the witness's preceding testimony.

"Doctor. Men's nervous structures and their reactions are as different as their physiognomies, are they not?"

"People differ a great deal—yes, sir."

"And many factors must be taken into consideration by the scientist in determining just how the nerves and muscles of a man—any given man—will react under different forms of shock?"

"That's very true."

"Thank you, Doctor. I, too, have no more questions."

"That is all. You may be excused," voiced the District Attorney.

After Doctor Webb left the stand, Judge Freeman commented, "It's late. We'll take a recess until tomorrow morning at ten o'clock. I admonish the jury not to discuss this case amongst yourselves or with anyone else during that time."

As court recessed and the spectators filed out the double doors in the rear of the courtroom, Bill Keys had a chance to confer briefly with his attorneys and with his wife. Minutes later he was escorted out of the room by two deputies to his cell in the Riverside jail.

XIII

July 15, 1943
Thursday

Ray H. Pinker was the prosecution's next witness, as court reconvened on the sixth day. As a result of questioning by the District Attorney, the forensic chemist told of examining Bill Keys' clothing that he had supposedly worn on the day of the shooting.

"I made an examination with a microscope of the stained areas in the clothing, testing them with benzedine reagent. I found no blood on the clothing."

"Did you make an examination, Mr. Pinker, of the clothing worn by the deceased at the time of his death?"

"I did."

"What was that examination?"

"Well, I made an examination of that clothing to determine the location of bloodstains. I wanted to see whether or not there were any blood stains on the trousers that would indicate that the body had been in more than one position."

"Now with particular reference to the blue denim trousers, did you find any blood stains on them?"

"Yes, I did. But I found no blood stains below the belt line of the trousers with the exception of a small blood stain on the outer surface of the rear left pocket—and an occasional small blood stain on the back of the lower legs."

"And with reference to the shirt of the deceased?"

"There are large stains of blood. Mixed in with the blood were tissue and sand."

"Now, Mr. Pinker, directing your attention to the fifteenth of May, this year, did you go to Twentynine Palms in San Bernardino County?"

"I did."

"With whom?"

"With yourself and Albert Kelley."

"Upon our arrival in Twentynine Palms, did you examine an automobile at a public garage for blood stains?"

"I did. It was a Victory Dodge with California license plates number 6A2029, supposedly the property of the defendant, William F. Keys."

"Now, will you tell the jury what kind of examination that you made on that car, Mr. Pinker?"

"Well, first I looked for blood stains, but I found none anywhere on the automobile. Next, I made an examination of the car for bullet marks. I found a mark that resembled a ricochet mark on the edge of the door on the driver's side. I examined this mark carefully first with the door open and then with it closed. The mark showed that the damage had been caused by a small object of appreciable velocity striking the edge of the door, bending the metal and chipping off the paint while the door was in an open position. Using a small hand magnifier, I also found some debris that looked like lead. This I removed to take to the laboratory for analysis."

"What did you do with this debris, Mr. Pinker?"

"I made a spectrochemical analysis of the debris to determine its chemical composition. I found it to be composed principally of lead alloyed with antimony. There was also present small amounts of calcium, magnesium and silicum."

"Did you also receive a .38 calibre revolver from Deputy Walwrath which belonged to the deceased, Worth Bagley?"

"I did on the fifteenth of May, 1943."

"At the time you received that revolver were there cartridges in it?"

"Yes. There were five cartridges in it, and also one fired shell which Deputy Walwrath had taken out and given me just a few minutes prior to turning the revolver over to me."

"Did you make a spectrochemical analysis of the lead in that cartridge?"

"I did—two of them. I found the alloy composition to be the same as the debris which I had removed from the ricochet mark on the automobile belonging to the defendant."

"And with respect to the four cartridges taken from the defendant's .30/.30 Remington rifle, did you make any similar analysis of them?"

"Yes. I selected one of the two cartridges having the bullets with soft lead noses and made a spectrochemical analysis of it. I found its composition to be principally lead alloyed with copper, and also a trace of silver, but there was no antimony."

"Mr. Pinker, did you compare that with the debris that you had removed from the car?"

"I did. It was of a different composition."

"And what is your conclusion with respect to this comparison that you made?"

"It is my opinion that the mark on the car door was a ricochet mark from a fired bullet of the same composition as the bullets or the cartridges in the .38 caliber revolver. Also, this mark was made on the car door at the time when the car door was open."

"With respect to Plaintiff's Exhibit M, the .38 caliber revolver, did you make an examination of that revolver?"

"I did. I made an examination to ascertain whether or not the revolver had been fired. I found residues in the barrel and gas blast markings in the opening of the cylinder that in my opinion, indicates that this revolver had been fired in the position in which I found the fired shell."

"I also made a further examination to determine what the trigger pull of the gun was in a cocked position and found that it was two to two and a half pounds. I then conducted experiments, after removing the debris from the barrel with the gun in a cocked position, to determine whether or not the jarring effect of dropping the gun to the ground would cause the gun to fire. This time, I found that if the hammer struck a solid object, such as the ground, it would fire."

"Is a two and a half pound trigger pull, in your experience, a light or heavy pull?"

"In my experience, it is an extremely light trigger pull. Trigger pulls go as high as eight and nine pounds while the average is somewhere in the vicinity of three and a half to four pounds."

"Could this revolver be fired by pressing the hammer?"

"Yes, by striking the hammer in a cocked position. It would not, however, fire from a simple jar on the ground, unless the hammer actually struck the ground."

"Now Mr. Pinker, after you made your examination of the defendant's car in Twentynine Palms, did you go to the Bagley ranch in Joshua Tree National Monument?"

"Yes, I did, on the same day."

"At the time that you went there, did you have in your possession copies of some photographs taken at the scene of the shooting?"

"Yes, that's correct. I used them to make my investigation."

"And what kind of investigation did you make there?"

"I searched for the location of blood stains on the ground and on the plants at the spot where the body had been found as well as the adjacent area."

"From the photographs that you had at that time, were you able to locate the approximate position of the body with respect to those blood stains?"

"Yes, sir. I was able to orient the position of the body with reference to the blood stains by a comparison of the bushes and weeds, as shown in the photographs, and the position of those weeds with relation to the blood stains. I removed samples of this contaminated material to take back to my laboratory."

"What findings did you arrive at with respect to that growth?"

"I found a large blood stain on the vegetative growth sidewise from the position of the body, as well as a contamination of heavily mixed tissue, bone and sand. I also found other stains of blood. An examination of some of these stains showed an elliptical elongation. This indicated

87

that the direction in which the blood had struck the vegetative debris was parallel to the ground. Examination of the tissue, sand and bone mixture showed this debris to have been wrapped around the vertical twig in the horizontal direction—that is, approximately parallel to the ground."

"Mr. Pinker. With the court's permission and Counsel's indulgence, can you show the jury that debris through this microscope?" the District Attorney asked, pointing to the instrument being set up on a table in front of the jury box.

"Yes, and may I also suggest that those with glasses try looking at it both with and without their glasses. If the eyepieces are not properly adjusted for each person's eyes, they can be easily done so like a pair of binoculars."

The jury members filed out one at a time to look at the slide with the blood sample, after which they returned to their seats.

"Would you mind telling the jury what they are seeing?" added the District Attorney.

"Well, the stem is viewed running from left to right under the microscope. On the surface of this stem may be seen a reddish-brown spot which is approximately pear-shaped. This is a drop of blood, and we are looking at a stain comprised of many corpuscles whose shape indicates direction."

"And what was that direction?"

"That direction is approximately parallel with the surface of the ground—crosswise. The stems were growing approximately vertical."

"By that, do you mean that the stains that appear on this exhibit came from a direction parallel to the ground, rather than dropping from above? Is that correct?" the District Attorney emphasized.

"That is right."

"Now, Mr. Pinker, after your investigation and examination at the scene of the shooting, did you go to the home of the defendant, William Keys?"

"Yes, sir. I went into his home to make further investigations."

"Did you remove anything from the defendant's house?"

"I did. I removed a pair of general work trousers which I had found draped over an overstuffed chair in the living room."

"Do you have those trousers with you?"

"Yes, I have."

The witness reached under his chair, retrieving a paper bag which he had placed there when he had first come to the stand. From the bag he removed a pair of tan trousers which he handed to the District Attorney.

"I will ask that these be marked for identification," Neblett requested, holding them up for the court clerk to see. "Now, Mr. Pinker. At the time that you removed these trousers was the belt still in them?"

"Yes, sir—just as it appears here."

"Did the trousers appear then, as they do now?"

"Yes, they did with the following exceptions. There are certain stains on the trousers which I have located by encircling with ink, while other stains have been cut out of the fabric."

"After obtaining these trousers from the defendant's house, what did you do with them?"

"I took them to the laboratory to make a microscopic examination of the stains, as well as chemical and serological tests. As a result, I found the stains to be human blood."

"Were you able to determine from your examination, the direction of the blood splatter which caused these stains?"

"I was. There were twelve droplet-size stains on the left trouser leg and twenty-six on the right one extending from the crotch down to a point approximately eight inches from the cuff. These stains were on the inside of the leg and are from left to right and upward."

"Now, Mr. Pinker, did you form any opinion as to the age of these stains?"

"Well, I know of no method of determining the age of a blood stain. However, from a study of the character of these stains, I can state that they occurred since the last time that the trousers had been laundered, and they have not been appreciably worn since the stains got on them. This is indicated by the fact that they have not been absorbed into the fabric but are surface stains. They're small droplets, dried and caught in the nap and in the upper surface of the fabric. A mere brushing or rough treatment of the surface would cause them to chip off and break away. Consequently, those trousers have not been worn enough to damage those stains since the time that they were contaminated," the forensic chemist stated.

Frances Keys listened closely as the District Attorney tried to convince the jury that her husband had been wearing these tan trousers at the time of the shooting. As soon as Pinker handed them to John Neblett, she knew that they could not have been the ones. Bill always saved his tan ones for his trips to Indio to get hay or when they went into Twentynine Palms or Banning for supplies. "Why, he'd never take a chance on ruining a good pair of pants doing work chores," she thought, "and he never wears a belt with his work clothes either." As far as explaining the origin of those bloodstains, that was easy. Like one of their daughters, Bill was afflicted with frequent nosebleeds. Many a night she had awakened to find him sitting on the edge of their bed, bent over with a pool of blood on the wooden floor. At these times, she had put a wet towel on the back of his neck to stop the bleeding. She was sure that Bill would mention this to his counsel, but in case he didn't, she sure would so that the District Attorney wouldn't get away with this misinformation. Then her thoughts returned to the proceedings, as John Neblett was about to conclude with his witness.

"Now, Mr. Pinker. As a result of your examination of the blood stains at the scene of the shooting, the photographs which were then in your possession, the gun, and clothing of the deceased, and the testimony regarding the infiltration of sand and foreign matter into the wound of the deceased, did you form any opinion with regard to the position of the deceased at the time he received the fatal wound?"

"Yes, I did. It is my opinion that at the time the victim received the wound in the arm and lower abdomen, that he was lying in a position prone on the ground," Pinker said without any hesitation.

"Thank you, Mr. Pinker. Your witness, counsel."

"One moment, counsel," interrupted the judge. "It's after recess time. We will take a recess until two o'clock. I will admonish the jurors as before not to converse among yourselves nor with anyone else about this case."

The courtroom emptied, while Bill talked quietly with his attorneys about Pinker's testimony. A few minutes later, Frances joined them.

When court reconvened at two o'clock, Judge Freeman announced that a matter had come up necessitating an adjournment until the next morning.

"The jury may be excused until tomorrow morning at ten o'clock," he said.

After saying goodbye to her husband, Frances left the room with Daisy Kiler for the drive back to Alhambra. She had seen the District Attorney's determination to prove Bill was guilty. In her own mind, she knew he wasn't. She hoped that Paul D'Orr would be able to counter the evidence that was being weighed against him.

XIV

July 16, 1943
Friday

Judge Freeman made another unexpected announcement a few minutes after court reconvened the next morning. Due to the illness of several jurors, he had decided, after conferring with both attorneys, to postpone the trial proceedings for the day. He admonished the jury members about discussing the case, then the sound of his gavel adjourned the court until the following Tuesday at ten o'clock.

Plate 1

Plate 2

Plate 3

Plate 4

Plate 5

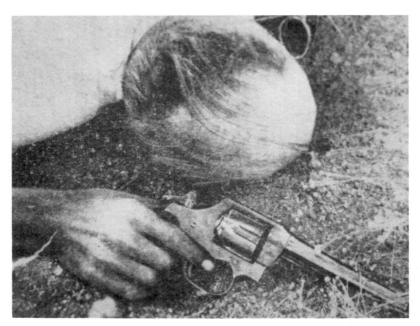

Plate 6

Plate 7

Plate 8

Plate 9

Plate 10

Plate 11

Plate 12

ate 13

Plate 14

Plate 15

Plate 16

Plate 1. *Alfred MacArthur and Bill Keys in 1908.* Sent out by million-aire Alfred Johnson, MacArthur discovered Death Valley Scotty's rich gold mine to be a hoax. MacArthur was the brother of Charles MacArthur, famous playwright who was married to actress Helen Hayes. Photo courtesy of the Keys family.

Plate 2. *The young Keys family in the early 1930's.* Photo courtesy of the Keys family.

Plate 3. *Bill Keys heading out to one of his mining claims.* Always interested in mining, Bill managed to find time to slip away from the rigors of keeping his ranch going in order to prospect in the mountains nearby. Photo courtesy of the Keys family.

Plate 4. *Worth Bagley's Last Warning.* One of two cardboard signs that Bagley made to place in the roadway as Bill Keys crossed his property at the time of the ambush. Photo from author's collection.

Plate 5. *Stone marker along the old dirt road locates spot where Bagley died in a hail of gunfire.* Bill carved and erected the monument after his return from prison. Photo by the author.

Plate 6. *Bagley's body*, his right hand still firmly clutching his cocked .38 caliber Colt revolver. Photo from San Bernardino County Sheriff's Department.

101

Plate 7. Bagley's final resting place was many miles from where he died. World War I veteran Bagley's grave in the Los Angeles National Cemetery. Photo by the author.

Plate 8. *Frances Keys rereads one of Bill's letters from San Quentin.* Her faith in her husband's innocence kept Frances going during Bill's five and a half year absence. Her letter to old friend Erle Stanley Gardner prompted him to reopen the case. Photo courtesy of the Keys family.

Plate 9. *Frances marks October 25, 1948 on her calendar,* the day Bill is to be released from San Quentin. Photo courtesy of the Keys family.

Plate 10. *Home from prison.* Bill Keys (left) shows some of his ore samples to two visitors to his ranch. Raymond Schindler (right), a member of Erle Stanley Gardner's Court of Last Resort, was instrumental in uncovering new evidence in Bill's favor. The other man is believed to be Sam Hicks, Gardner's ranch foreman. Photo by Erle Stanley Gardner, courtesy of the Keys family.

Plate 11. Starting in 1949, Bill undertook several dam building projects at his ranch. His engineering skills were marveled at by professional engineers. Today his dams still hold water collected in the rain-fed lakes behind them. Photo courtesy of the Keys family.

Plate 12. *Frances Keys with one of her purple-glass dishes.* Through the years she built her collection into one of the finest in the area. Long exposure to the hot desert sun turned the glass manufactured prior to 1914 to the deep purple color. Photo courtesy of the Keys family.

Plate 13. Bill remained alone at the ranch after Frances' death in 1963. He entertained his many visitors with stories of his early mining days with Death Valley Scotty, as well as his infamous gunfight with Worth Bagley. Photo courtesy of the National Park Service.

Plate 14. Winter can also be cold in the desert. Bill and Frances stand on the frozen wash behind their house during the cold January of 1949. Photo courtesy of the Keys family.

Plate 15. *Gwyn and Willis Keys begin carving Bill's tombstone, Easter 1978.* Although he erected markers for the other members of his family buried at the ranch, Bill never did one for himself. Ranger friends erected a stone that he had cut, while Willis and Gwyn completed its carving with inlaid blue stones that Bill had saved from some of his mining trips. Photo by the author.

Plate 16. Bill and Frances' ranch house still stands through winter snows and desert heat. Lack of funds by the National Park Service for restoration have doomed the house, ranch and its machinery to slow disintegration despite high popularity of the ranger-conducted ranch tours. Photo by the author, January 1979.

102

XV

July 20, 1943
Tuesday

The eighth day of testimony began when court reconvened and Ray H. Pinker resumed his seat on the witness stand. After checking his notes taken during the previous testimony, Defense Attorney Paul D'Orr walked to his place before the witness and began his cross-examination.

"Mr. Pinker, did you make only one trip out to the scene of the shooting?"

"Yes, sir—just one trip."

"Did you examine the body of the deceased at Banning?"

"No. At no time have I seen the body of the deceased."

"Now, Mr. Pinker, you stated in this court earlier that you made certain tests as a result of your examination of the deceased's revolver. Are those the only examinations that you made?"

"Well, I also examined the barrel of the revolver and removed some fine sand which I found adhered to a greasy residue in the barrel."

"Now this court has heard prior testimony from Deputy Worchester that no fingerprints were found on this revolver when it was examined. Do you know from what the stock or side of the butt of this revolver was formed?"

"Yes, sir. I believe it's wood—it has a rough surface."

"You gentlemen call the impressions left by oil and sweat of the human hand, latent fingerprints or latent prints. Is that not right?"

"Yes, that's correct."

"Could latent prints have been on that revolver?"

"No. The grips on that gun could not possibly hold a latent palm print or fingerprint, because of the very texture or nature of its surface. It's necessary to have a more or less smooth surface before a latent palm or fingerprint will adhere to it. The surface must be clean too. If it's an oily surface, a latent fingerprint will not adhere."

D'Orr considered this answer a moment before framing his next question.

"What about the use of silver nitrate or iodine fuming to make latent prints visible?"

"No. I wouldn't say wood is very good for either method. I have known several cases where the silver nitrate method was used. The Lindberg kidnapping case is one example where a wooden ladder was given a bath in silver nitrate in order to render the chlorides present in the perspiration of the fingers to become visible."

"I understand that method was used. When it was used, it produced numerous fingerprints, although none of them happened to be Hauptmann's," commented the defense attorney.

"Yes. None of them happened to be Lindberg's either, and he handled that ladder more than anyone else."

"That's right. That's one of the great fingerprint mysteries," added Paul D'Orr. "I think that's all the questions I have of this witness."

After the forensic chemist was excused, District Attorney Neblett stood up from his chair and said, "We rest, your Honor."

Paul D'Orr walked back to the table where his assistant, Thomas Reynolds, was seated next to Bill Keys. After a moment's consultation with them, he walked back toward the front of the courtroom and called Bill as his first witness. Bill was sworn in and his testimony began.

"Mr. Keys, what is your age?"

"Sixty-three."

"Where do you live?"

"I live out in the eastern portion of San Bernardino County at my ranch."

"How long have you been out there in that neighborhood?"

"Thirty-three years."

"Are you married?"

"Yes. We have four children. The oldest is a boy and the other three are girls."

"What are their ages?"

"Twenty-one, eighteen, fourteen, and twelve."

"What has been your occupation in those mountains?"

"Mining and raising stock."

"How many acres do you own?"

"Well, I have eight hundred acres—part are in Riverside County but my home is in San Bernardino County."

"Now, Mr. Keys, have you a mine in this general neighborhood anywhere?"

"Yes, the Desert Queen. It would be in Section six of Riverside County."

"All right. And how long have you been working that mine?"

"Since 1910."

"Do you know about how long Mr. Bagley had been in this neighborhood?"

"Yes, about five or six years. I don't know exactly."

"How far is his house from yours—as the crow flies?"

"About two miles."

"Now do you have a pumping plant in Riverside County?"

"Yes, I do."

"And where is it located?"

"It's just north of the Bagley ranch. It's reached one way by a road running through part of the Bagley property."

"What does that pumping plant and mill, as it is called, consist of?"

"Well, there's a two-stamp mill and a reduction plant for reducing gold ore—that is, breaking up the ore and concentrating it."

"What other machinery is there?"

"A gasoline engine, concentrating tables, a pump, a well, a tank, and two cattle troughs."

"How much will the troughs hold apiece?

"They hold three hundred gallons together."

"And the tank?"

"It holds five hundred gallons."

"Where is it located?"

"It's right by the well between the trough and the well."

D'Orr paused while his assistant set up a large map of this desert area in front of the courtroom. In this position it could be easily seen, both by the witness and the jury members.

"Now Mr. Keys. Let's confine our attention to this road which goes through the Bagley ranch to your pumping plant," he said, pointing to the route on the map. "How long has it existed?"

"Since 1874," came the defendant's reply.

"Did you ever operate a mill, or have a mill at any other point other than at the pumping plant of which we just spoke?"

"Yes, sir. I have a mill at my place."

"When you were operating the Desert Queen Mine some years ago, where did you get water?"

"I got water at my home place where the five-stamp mill is located."

"Calling your attention to this well here, now known as the Bagley well," he said, pointing to the location on the map, "did you ever pump at this well?"

"Oh, yes—from 1910 until about 1936."

"After Mr. Bagley bought his land from the Southern Pacific Railroad, what did you do about the old well? Did you have any machinery on it?"

"Yes, sir. I had a windmill, tank, and engine which I took off."

"And you never attempted to pump water at that well any longer?"

"No, I did not," Bill said definitely.

"How did you obtain the Desert Queen Mine? Was that government land?"

"No, I bought that."

"Now Mr. Keys, from the time that you started to work the Desert Queen Mine, over how long a period was it that this land was not occupied—that is the Bagley ranch?"

"Up to 1936."

"When did you remove your machinery?"

"Well, I think it was around '35."

"By the way, prior to the time Mr. Bagley bought that property, did what we call the Bagley well have any other name?"

"Yes, it was called the Desert Queen Well."

"At the time you bought the Desert Queen Mine, were there any water rights connected with the mine or rights to the use of any well?"

"Yes, the Desert Queen Well."

"And you abandoned it when Mr. Bagley bought this land?"

"Yes, sir. I did."

D'Orr left the map and walked back to stand directly in front of Bill. "Now will you please tell the court the first time that you met Worth Bagley?"

"Well, let's see—I first met him in Queen Valley—that's the valley just east of the Bagley ranch. He inquired about some survey stakes and told me that he was about to buy some land nearby. I showed him where the stakes were. The next time I saw him, he was coming through my ranch with a trailer loaded with one thing or another."

"Did you make any objection to his traveling on the road that goes across your ranch?"

"No, sir. I didn't."

"When did your next conversation with him take place?"

Bill thought for a moment before speaking.

"Sometime in 1937—I was out in the yard at my place when he drove up to where I was working on a fence and started talking. In the conversation, he said he was from the Los Angeles Sheriff's Office, that he had bought some land, and that he intended to live out there for his health. As we talked there for a little while, he mentioned being a man that 'pulled people's noses.' Well, I didn't say anything to that. We talked about the fence, and that was all."

"Mr. Keys, do you remember another conversation that same year?"

"Oh yes. He came to my ranch home alone, and we talked out in the yard. He told me that I had his windmill, and he wanted me to bring it back, and to put it up on his land where I had gotten it. I told him that I wouldn't, that his land had formerly been owned by the Southern Pacific Railroad, and that they had given me thirty days to remove my personal belongings—so therefore, I had removed my windmill."

"When was the next occasion that you can recall any contact with Mr. Bagley?"

Again Bill paused to think about the question.

"Let's see—well, we were looking for stakes in the southeast corner of Section four. We had found the quarter corner and were measuring back when he drove up in a truck to where I was standing at the corner post. I was sighting through while the other boys, who were with me at the south stake, were trying to determine where the line was. Anyway, Bagley drove up. He had a rifle sitting alongside of him and a revolver on his belt. He said to me, 'I have established that line. You needn't try to establish any more.' Well, I told him that I wanted to be sure, and that the boys on the hill would be checking it anyway."

"Is that about the extent of the conversation?" inquired D'Orr.

"Well, that was all that was said about the line, because a man named Geil drove up. A woman came running from Bagley's house to meet him. I didn't know the woman, but they talked a little while."

"Did you indicate by your voice or actions, any hostility toward Mr. Bagley?"

"No, I didn't."

"All right. Now, when was the next time you saw or talked to him?"

"Well, that would have been sometime in late June or early July of 1938. I was on horseback out on the main Monument road, when he drove up in his truck. He said that my cattle were coming up to his house and bothering him, that they were vicious, and that he was not going to allow it. So I told him I would build a fence to block off his house. He said all right, and that he would see me later. Then he drove on."

"Before we go on, Mr. Keys, perhaps you had better explain to us about your cattle," said the defense attorney. "How many head of cattle did you have in 1936, 1937, 1938, and down to the present time?"

"Well at present, there are around 150. Previously, there was a smaller number, as I sold some stock each year and bought some. In the winter, I graze my cattle in Pleasant Valley, which is south of Queen Valley. In the summer they graze in Lost Horse Valley, which is west of Queen Valley and the Bagley ranch."

"How many times a year do you move those cattle?"

"Twice—in the fall around the first of December, and in the spring sometime from May first until sometime in June. I move them along the road that goes through Bagley's place. They drift up toward my millsite to get water then out into Queen Valley. If it's in the fall, they go down into Pleasant Valley."

"So you agreed to build a fence to keep your cattle out of part of the Bagley ranch. When did you see him again?"

Once again Bill paused to consider D'Orr's question before answering.

"Let's see—that would have been about ten days later, in July 1938, when he came up to my pumping station at the mill. I had a man named Lawrence and his son working for me up there. They were working on my well when Bagley drove up. Mr. Lawrence went out to talk to him. When he came back, he told me that Bagley wanted us to start on the fence."

"So what did you do?"

"We proceeded to build a two-strand barbed wire fence around approximately eighty acres of his property. It ran from the rocks south of the Bagley house and came around through the valley up to his well. From there it turned northward to the rocks."

"Let me see if I have this correct, Mr. Keys. Since his house was back against a shelf of rocks, the effect of that fence was to block off the territory in the cove?"

"Yes, sir."

"Who paid for the wire, the posts, and other materials?"

"I did."

"And who did the work?"

"Myself, Mr. Lawrence and his son."

"Now, how long after the fence was built, was that road used in moving cattle from one range to the other?"

"Well, it was understood that when we completed the fence, I would be able to move my cattle freely through the grounds from one range to the other, as well as to also use the road that went to my mill."

"And again these roads have been used by the public since when?"

"1874," came Bill's definite reply.

"Fine. So when did you next see Mr. Bagley?"

"Just after we finished the fence. I asked him if he was satisfied with it. He said yes, it was all right, but he wanted a cattle guard and one gate. So we built them. The gate was on the south end of the fence line and the cattle guard was over near his well."

"How often did you use that road, Mr. Keys?"

"Just about every day," came his reply, as he changed his position in the hard-backed chair in an attempt to get more comfortable.

"When was the next time that you saw Worth Bagley?"

"Well, a few weeks later I found one of my cows down near his property line and the road that goes on to Twenty-nine Palms. My brother-in-law was with me. Upon probing the wound, he discovered she had been shot and the bullet was still in her. We also saw a man and a woman's footprints near the body. A few days later, Bagley and his wife came over to our house."

"Who was present there?"

"My wife, the two Lawrence boys, and myself."

"When you saw Mr. Bagley on this occasion, did any conversation take place?"

110

"Yes. Bagley said, 'Excuse my hand, my arm's paralyzed. I've been pensioned off, and I expect to live out here permanently.' Then he said that he had been taken to the Riverside Hospital and to a hospital in Los Angeles, because he had been found wandering around the streets. He thought that he had been mentally unbalanced at the time. Then, as he was getting into his truck to leave, my wife accused him of shooting my cattle."

"What did he do then?"

"He immediately gave his truck the gas and pulled out of our yard."

"When was your next meeting with Worth Bagley?"

"That would have been about two weeks later. I was on my way to Twentynine Palms and was over near Bagley's property when I saw a pool of blood in the road. I got out to examine it. About that time Bagley and his wife drove up behind me, and he got out. When I pointed to the blood, Bagley told me that he had killed a dog there the night before. Then he said, 'You've accused me of shooting your cattle. Don't never accuse me of that again or the next time I shoot, it won't be cattle.'"

"Did you make any reply?"

"Well, I walked up a little closer toward him. I looked him in the eye for a moment. He backed away, heading back to his truck. I followed him over to it and saw Mrs. Bagley. She said, 'We saw your cattle on the road.' I said, 'Yes, they're everywhere.' And that was the end of our conversation, as they drove off."

Paul D'Orr paused to allow the jury time to reflect on his client's testimony before proceeding. "Now, Mr. Keys. Can you recall any other conversations with your neighbor, Worth Bagley?"

"A couple of months later my brother-in-law, Lansing Lawton and I found one of my mules, a Spanish Jack, shot on my property just a short distance from Bagley's south line. We looked for the bullet but couldn't find it, so we did cut out a piece of the hide where the bullet had entered the body. A few days later we met Bagley in Queen Valley. This time I accused him of killing the Spanish Jack, an animal

111

that was worth $250. He denied it, but said, 'Well, when I shoot again, it won't be animals.' When he said this, he looked threatening. His eyes were very excited, and he became very angry. I also noticed that he had his gun with him."

"Did you say anything in reply to his statement?"

"No. I don't believe I did."

"All right, Mr. Keys. Now I have another question for you. About how far is it from Twentynine Palms to the entrance of Bagley's ranch and then down to your own ranch?"

"Why, that's about twenty-two miles."

"Is that road over which you say Mr. Bagley had free access across your property, a part of the route that would be taken to his ranch?"

"Yes, it would."

"Tell us who built that road."

"Well, that was an old road when I first came out there, but I improved it and made part of it."

"Did Mr. Bagley ever do any hauling over that road that went through your place?"

"Oh yes. He hauled all of his material over it."

"Did you ever object to it?"

"No, sir."

"Now when was the next time that you met Mr. Bagley?"

Bill hesitated for a moment, trying to get the events straight in his mind before he spoke. "Well, in 1940, I was working for the National Monument. I went over to Bagley's ranch with a Park Service surveyor whose name was Charlie. I was helping him to locate the section lines that he was surveying. That day we had a third man with us by the name of Connors. We had driven over from Quail Springs, opened the west gate into the Bagley place, then drove up to his house."

"After you got there, did the surveyor have any conversation with Mr. Bagley?"

"Yes, sir. Charlie said we had come up there for the purpose of surveying as well as to look for a certain stake corner."

112

"And what did you say?"

"Nothing. Bagley was standing on his porch, and I was sitting in the back seat of the car. When he saw me, he pointed to me and said, 'Bill Keys can tell you where that stake is.' The surveyor answered, 'All right.' He unloaded the heavy instrument, giving it to us. I stepped out on the opposite side from where Bagley was, took the big instrument, and set it up in front of the car. The surveyor remained at the front door. In the meantime Bagley had gone into the house but all of a sudden he came out the door and ran towards me all excited-like. The surveyor stepped in between us, as Bagley said, 'Don't never bring Bill Keys on my land again.'"

"Did you make any reply to this?"

"No, sir. I did nothing at all."

"Now Mr. Keys, did anyone ever communicate to you any threats that Bagley had made against you, and if so, will you please tell the court about them?"

"Yes, Mr. Boyee, who was working at a mine near Bagley's place, told me about one. We had gone to Los Angeles in his automobile. On the way there, he told me, 'Bagley said he was going to kill you, and that it would be in the near future.' He warned me that I had better look out and arm myself."

"And your neighbor, Mrs. Heddington? Did she make any statement to you with reference to having talked with Bagley?"

"Yes. She looked me straight in the eye and said, 'You will surely have to watch that man.'"

"Did she tell you anything that he had said?"

"No, she didn't."

"I move the answer be stricken out," voiced the District Attorney, rising quickly from his seat.

"That may go," D'Orr replied.

"Strike it out," Judge Freeman advised the court reporter, and the District Attorney resumed his seat.

"Now Mr. Keys. Do you recollect the first time that you found any logs, other obstructions, or barricades across any part of this road near the Bagley well, or on the one to your Wall Street Mill?"

"Yes, sir. It was the latter part of 1941 or in the beginning of 1942."

"Prior to that time had you had any difficulty or dispute with Mr. Bagley?"

"None other than what I had mentioned."

"You had not seen him?"

"No, sir."

"All right, please tell us what you found at that time."

"Well, on my way to my mill, I found a yucca lying in the middle of the road, which I removed."

"When was the next time that you found any obstructions on your mill road?"

"It was sometime in January of this year. It looked like broken bottles—broken up in sharp shapes and set into the ground. I found it just above the junction on the road leading from the Bagley well."

"Over how much of the roadway did this broken glass extend?"

"Well, it was across both tracks. I took one of the other roads alongside of it."

"All right, we'll leave that for the time being. In 1940, after the occasions that you have referred to, and the communications made by Mr. Bagley to you in a talk with Mr. Boyee, did you communicate with any law enforcement agency of Riverside County—I mean by letter or otherwise?"

"Yes, sir. I did."

D'Orr walked over to his table, returning with some papers. "Counsel, I imagine that you have seen this letter?" he said, handing it to the District Attorney.

As Neblett began to look over this new piece of evidence, Judge Freeman interrupted.

"Counsels, before we continue, we might as well break for lunch at this time."

*   *   *   *   *

114

After the recess, the members of the jury resumed their seats. When both counsels and the defendant were present, the trial continued. Instead of recalling Bill Keys to the stand, Paul D'Orr had other plans for the afternoon session. He stood to address the court.

"If the Court please, I have two or three witnesses here who have come from distances under subpoena to produce records. They are, as always, exceedingly anxious to return to their regular duties. One of these witnesses, Mr. Veit, represents the United States government. The Veterans Administraton has sent him in answer to a subpoena issued out of this court to produce certain hospitalization records of and concerning Worth Bagley at the Sawtelle Hospital. This witness, if placed on the stand, will call your Honor's attention to the law under which the Veterans Administration cannot be compelled to produce those records except perhaps under a subpoena from a United States Court. We therefore have made up our minds that we cannot compel him to produce them and are willing that this witness be excused."

The District Attorney interrupted, "I might state, your Honor, even if such records were produced, the prosecution would object on the grounds that such records are hearsay. Therefore, I have no objection to this witness being excused."

"Mr. Veit. You may be excused," came the judge's order.

"Thank you, your Honor."

As the excused witness left the courtroom, Paul D'Orr continued, "Counsel makes no point of the order of proof. As I stated to your Honor, I have other witnesses who are actually armed with records. At this time I should like to call Deputy Sheriff C. W. Lee to the witness stand."

From his seat in the back of the courtroom the lawman walked forward to take his seat and be sworn in by the bailiff. Then Paul D'Orr revealed why this witness had been called.

"Mr. Lee. Please tell me what your occupation or profession is."

"I am an accountant for the Los Angeles County Sheriff's

Department. I'm also deputized as a Deputy Sheriff within that Department."

"What are your duties and functions?"

"I have charge of the accounting and financial division of the Sheriff's Department. In conjunction with that, I act as secretary to the Los Angeles Peace Officers Retirement System."

"Now, Mr. Lee, you have come here in answer to the court's subpoena to produce certain records?"

"Yes, I have," he answered, looking down at the large file he held in his lap.

"Will you tell us, without indicating the contents of the documents, what those records are?"

"Yes, sir. This file has the application for retirement by Worth Bagley for disability, the action of the Retirement Board on his application, and various doctor's statements regarding the physical examination, as well as the condition of Mr. Bagley at the time that he was retired."

"Are you the proper custodian of those records?"

"Yes."

"Are you able to identify them?"

"Yes, sir. I am."

"Were those reports and supporting papers upon which the action of the Retirement Board was based?"

"Yes, sir. They are. The application was prepared by the applicant for retirement and sustained by his physician's medical report. Other reports were prepared by the doctors appointed by the Board for the applicant's physical examination prior to his actual approval or disapproval by the Board of his retirement."

"And are those records that you have with you public records of Los Angeles County?"

"Yes, sir."

"Very well, Mr. Lee. Please produce for me the application of Worth Webster Bagley, supporting examinations and diagnoses of the three physicians, the minutes of the Board, telling us the dates of each."

The witness opened the file folders on his lap and extracted the asked-for documents.

"Here is the application dated December 2, 1938. I have one doctor's report of December 13, 1938, and then the Board's physicians' reports each dated October 10, 1939."

"What is the date of the minutes of the Board's action?"

"That date is November 22, 1939."

"Do the records show that the deceased was retired by reasons of those proceedings?"

"Yes, sir. They do."

D'Orr then addressed the judge. "Your Honor. The court has already heard me express my willingness to prove certain facts. These documents are offered in proof of those facts, pertaining to the conduct of the defendant as a reasonable man in what he did at the time of the final affray."

Neblett once again jumped up from his seat to offer resistance. "I object to the admission of these documents on the following grounds: First, they are incompetent, irrelevant and immaterial, and do not tend to prove or disprove any of the issues in this case. Second, there is no sufficient foundation laid as to the purported application of Worth Bagley. And third, the supporting statements of the doctors are pure hearsay. The doctors are not present to be subjected to cross-examination."

The District Attorney walked forward toward the judge's bench to continue his argument further. "Your Honor, I have not read these instruments, but the very nature of them would indicate that they are hearsay. As far as the dates at which application was taken, or the fact that the deceased was retired on a certain date—I have no objection to that. I do object to the records themselves when they contain the conclusions of physicians who are not present, the action of the Board, and the reasons thereof, which would be pure conclusions and therefore would be hearsay."

Judge Freeman gave his ruling almost immediately. "Objection sustained. You may mark these for identification," he stated, indicating the records brought by the witness.

Paul D'Orr did not seem to be taken back by the ruling.

"Thank you, Mr. Lee. The Clerk of the Court will be ordered to return these records to the Sheriff's office in Los

117

Angeles in care of you. You may be excused. Now, I would like to call Mrs. Esther Johnson as the next witness for the defense."

The Medical Records Librarian from the Riverside County Hospital took her place on the witness stand. She was sworn in and D'Orr began his questioning.

"Young lady. Have you appeared in answer to the Court's subpoena to produce certain records from the Riverside County Hospital?"

"Yes, I have."

"Are these records kept under your supervision and within your custody as Medical Records Librarian there?"

"Yes, they are."

"Will you tell us what they contain without describing or reciting any of their contents?"

"They are entrance records, personal history sheet, physical examination, laboratory reports, doctors' orders, nurses' notes, and some correspondence concerning Worth Bagley."

"Were all of these records made in the regular course of the case that they purport to cover?"

"They were."

"And these records cover what period of time?"

"February 18, 1939 to February 22, 1939."

"Do they relate totally to Worth Webster Bagley?"

"They do."

After these preliminary questions, D'Orr made his intended legal move.

"If the Court please, I offer these documents on the grounds heretofore indicated in the discussion with the Court and testified to by Mr. Keys, which he had with Worth Bagley about having been in Riverside Hospital, and that he was wandering around and didn't know what he was doing."

"To which we object!" Neblett voiced strongly. "We object on the grounds that the hospital records are not admissible to prove matters contained therein, and that the records are hearsay. As to the date of admission and the date of release, I have no objection. May I question your witness, Counsel?"

118

"Yes," replied D'Orr.

"Mrs. Johnson, did you make these records yourself with respect to the admission of the patient?"

"No."

"Were you present at the time the admission papers were filled out?"

"No."

"I therefore object, your Honor, on the grounds these records are hearsay. This witness did not prepare the records on which she is dependent. If these records go in, they are hearsay."

The defense attorney was equally as adamant as Neblett on this matter and was determined to have the records admitted into evidence.

"I admit that the witness would testify from the records, but to save further time, I now offer these records in evidence for the purposes heretofore indicated."

"Mr. D'Orr, are you making a motion that they be received in evidence?" questioned Judge Freeman.

"Yes. I am offering them in evidence, your Honor," came his affirmative reply.

"The motion is denied. They will be marked for identification and left with the Clerk here just the same as the others."

"This witness may be excused, as far as we are concerned," added the defense attorney, taken back by this setback.

"I think we'll take an adjournment until tomorrow morning at ten o'clock," pronounced the judge.

As the courtroom began to clear, Paul D'Orr returned to the defense table to gather up his papers and to confer quickly with Bill before he was returned to his cell in the Riverside jail. D'Orr's expression did not mirror the frustration that he felt after this last afternoon's proceedings. He knew that without these records, his work was cut out for him to show the jury the true character of the deceased, Worth Bagley. As he and his assistant, Thomas Reynolds, left the room, D'Orr promised himself a full night of research to prepare for the next day's session.

XVI

July 21, 1943
Wednesday

On the ninth day Paul D'Orr attempted to introduce medical affidavits relating to Bagley's physical and mental condition. Once again, the defense attorney met strong resistance from John Neblett as well as from Judge Freeman, who sustained the District Attorney's objection. In an attempt at new tactics, D'Orr called as his next witness Lansing Kendall Lawton, Bill Keys' brother-in-law, who was then on active duty with the United States Navy in Oakland, California.

After a number of preliminary questions concerning his Navy work and his relationship to Bill Keys, the defense attorney concentrated on the period from 1938 to 1940 when Lawton had been living at the Keys ranch.

"Were you present with the defendant at a time when he had any conversations with Worth Bagley?"

"Yes, I was. It was sometime in 1939."

"Mr. Lawton, do you remember distinctly the occasion of this conversation?"

"Yes. It took place on the Twentynine Palms road close to Bagley's and Mr. Keys' place."

"Can you tell us about the conversation?"

"Yes. The conversation was over a cow and a jack being killed. I think Mr. Keys expected some sort of settlement for those animals. He asked Bagley if he would make some sort of a settlement for the loss of his two animals. Well, Bagley flatly told him no. Then Mr. Keys asked him not to kill any more of his animals, to which Bagley replied that the next time that he killed anything, it wouldn't be animals."

"What was Bagley's appearance when he said that?"

"Well, he was pretty angry and wild-eyed."

"Do you remember whether or not at this time Mr. Bagley was armed?"

"He was always armed every time that I saw him—including this time," Lawton answered firmly.

"Did Mr. Keys make any hostile reply to this conversation?"

"No, he did not."

"Now when you were living at the Keys home were any statements brought to you of Mr. Bagley's threats to kill Mr. Keys or 'to get' Mr. Keys? Just answer this yes or no."

"Yes."

"Did you tell Mr. Keys or warn him that you had heard threats had been made against him?"

"Yes, sir. I did."

"Cross-examine."

The District Attorney proceeded from his usual position at the table to the front of the courtroom to begin cross-examination of the Navy Shipfitter, Second Class.

"Mr. Lawton. While you were at the Keys Ranch during 1938 through 1940, did Mr. Keys have more than one jack there?"

"Yes, I believe that he had two, although I'm not sure. They were usually out on the range."

"Do you recall a Mexican Jack being returned to Mr. Keys after this discussion?"

"The jack in this case was already dead and couldn't come back!" Lawton said firmly.

"Oh yes. During this conversation you stated that the defendant made no hostile reply to Mr. Bagley. Did he make any reply at all?"

"No, that ended the conversation. He started up the car and we left."

"After this conversation, did Mr. Keys communicate any threat to you against Mr. Bagley?"

"No, sir. He did not."

"During the time that you were with Mr. Keys at his ranch, what sort of work did you do?"

"Well, I helped him with the cattle at times and mined part of the time."

"Did you ride around in Mr. Keys' car with him?"

"Yes."

"At that time was Mr. Keys carrying a rifle in the car?"

"Why, he might have been carrying one. I don't remember."

"Do you recall whether he was carrying a rifle in his car on the date of that conversation with Mr. Bagley in Queen Valley?"

"There might have been one in the car, but he did not carry the rifle on his person."

"You mean he did not take it out of the car?" inquired the District Attorney.

"No. We were right in the car. It's a rough road out there. You have to turn out of that road to let another car pass."

"Mr. Lawton. Did he always carry that rifle in his car when he went over in the vicinity of the Bagley ranch?"

"Not necessarily, but when you work with cattle, it is customary . . . "

"I'm just referring to Mr. Keys and to those specific periods between 1939 and 1940," he interrupted.

"I would say there might have been a rifle in the car at any time, but I never checked that."

"I'm asking you if it was customary for Mr. Keys, during the period of 1939 and 1940, when he went into the vicinity of the Bagley ranch, to carry a rifle?" the District Attorney continued persistently.

Paul D'Orr interrupted. "That was asked and answered. The witness told us what he observed. You are asking what is customary, which seeks an opinion which he has stated."

But Lansing Lawton answered.

"I can't remember every time whether or not there was a rifle in the car. I've been in that car so many times. Sometimes there was a rifle, and sometimes there wasn't."

"That's all the questions the prosecution has for this

witness," Neblett stated before sitting down. Then D'Orr returned to the witness for redirect examination.

"Now Mr. Lawton, where was the body of this Spanish Jack when you saw it dead?"

"It was just off Mr. Bagley's property on Mr. Keys' land. Mr. Keys and I found it together."

"Very well, thank you, sir," said the defense attorney.

"That's all for us, also," replied Neblett.

"With the Court's permission, may this witness now return to the Armed Services of our country?" D'Orr addressed the bench.

"We have no objection," replied Judge Freeman.

With the official word, Lansing Lawton was excused from the witness stand. He walked past the defendant and to the back of the courtroom and sat down next to his sister, Frances, for the remainder of the day's sessions.

They watched a few minutes later, as Bill was recalled to the witness stand. He moved forward without his usual quick step. He didn't feel well and would be glad when this day's session was over. He was still plagued by a cold he had caught the day before. His swollen sinus had also affected his hearing. After he had taken his seat, Paul D'Orr's questions returned to the letter written by Mr. Keys to the former District Attorney in Riverside on June 10, 1940. The defense attorney had the letter in his hand, as he began his questioning.

"Mr. Keys, did you ask your wife to write this letter?"

"Yes, sir. I did."

"Did she include in this letter the suggestion that you gave her?"

"Yes, sir."

"Your Honor, I call your attention to the fact that this letter was written to the District Attorney of Riverside County, the county in which Mr. Bagley resided, and thus the proper county which had jurisdiction over this property. I think that the parts of the letter which we will read will show the anxiety that the defendant felt for himself to avoid violence and to resort to the constituted legal authorities."

123

John Neblett objected immediately. "If the Court please, we object to the admission of this letter into evidence on the grounds that it is incompetent, irrelevant, immaterial and self-serving. The contents of this letter go beyond what has already been established. They are conclusions, opinions, and are self-serving."

The two counsels argued the legal technicalities of the letter's admission while Judge Freeman questioned each point as it was raised. D'Orr argued that the letter was offered not to establish the truth about the charges against Bagley, but rather to show the state of mind of Bill Keys as being completely foreign to violence and actively seeking the assistance of the law. Judge Freeman considered both sides of the question before ruling that the court should be liberal. The defendant should be given the benefit of this evidence. As a result, D'Orr was then allowed to read certain portions of the letter to the jury.

He began reading, "Now whether this man is unbalanced mentally or just downright mean, something should be done about it, as he is a dangerous person to be at large."

He skimmed quickly over a paragraph or two of the letter before again reading out loud, "If your office can't do anything about this Bagley matter, you may be able to advise us what we can do, or what steps to take. We have no money to pay out for lawyers."

Then the last paragraph that he read was: "I would also like to know what the law is about stock getting onto a man's property that is not fenced or that is fenced. Has a man the right to shoot those animals? Also, will you please quote me that part of the trespass law that concerns people entering upon property that is posted with No Trespassing signs?"

The letter was marked for identification, after which the defense attorney returned to question Bill. When he asked him about his children's schooling, the defendant answered that they had gone to school at the ranch in a building which he had built; later the county had furnished the teachers. He explained that there had been several teachers during the ten years of the school's existence and that each had lived near

124

the family house in a cabin that he also had built. He concluded this discussion with the mention of Mrs. Dudley. She was the last teacher who had lived there with them until the school was discontinued the previous year. At that time his two youngest children were old enough to move to Alhambra to attend regular public school.

The subject of Worth Bagley was brought up once again. Bill said he had not seen Bagley during the last two years, although several people had told him that Bagley had threatened to kill him.

Paul D'Orr then returned to a question that had been brought up in the testimony of Constable Jack Cones.

"Mr. Keys, do you recollect going to Twentynine Palms some months before May 11th at which time you saw Constable Cones?"

"Yes, I went to see him two or three months before and ran into him at the gas station there."

"Please tell the jury from the beginning if you can, what was said at that meeting."

Bill cleared his throat before beginning. "I told him that the gate at the cattleguard at the junction of the Twentynine Palms-Quail Springs Road and the road going through Bagley's property was locked, and that Bagley was preventing me from driving my cattle through there. I wanted to know if that lock was illegal and couldn't be taken off so that I could use the public road which I was allowed to use. Well, Cones said that he didn't know anything about that. I answered that it was a narrow path about a quarter of a mile wide—a natural path—and I had to drive my cattle through there. I also mentioned about Bagley having put yuccas across the road at his ranch. Cones again said he couldn't do anything, because it was entirely out his county. Therefore he couldn't act in the matter. I think that was about all of the conversation."

"In that conversation did you tell Cones that you guessed you would have to shoot Bagley or words to that effect?"

"No, sir. I never did."

"Did you ever tell anybody that you were going to shoot Bagley?"

"No, never," he said again definitely.

"Did Mr. Cones make any statement about your going around the mountain—that is, driving your cattle all the way around?"

"No, he didn't. He did say that I might go to the law and get an injunction to have the gate opened. But he also said that he had had a talk with Bagley, and that he didn't like Bagley's actions or the talk that he had had with him. After this, Cones added, 'but that is all I can say to you.'"

"Again, you didn't tell Cones you guessed that you would have to shoot Bagley?'

"I did not!" he said definitely.

"Now Mr. Keys, did you ever tear down any gates or break any fences that Mr. Bagley had erected?"

"No."

"How often did you use that road?"

"I only drove my cattle through about twice a year and used the road when I went to my mill."

"Now, Mr. Keys, during the month of May who was with you at your home ranch?"

"Well, I had a couple of Indian boys from Mission Creek up there to help me with the cattle. My wife and children were living in Alhambra ever since school started. Willis and Virginia were working, while Patricia and Phyllis, the youngest, were going to school."

For the next ninety minutes the defense attorney took Bill slowly through the events of May 11th. His questions were exact so that nothing that happened to Bill that day was overlooked. In response to these questions, Bill said that it had been about a week since he had been at the millsite. Then on the morning of May 11th he had decided to go there to pump water for his cattle. On the way in he had seen nothing unusual. There was nothing in the road to indicate that anyone had been around. He told of his pumping water into his tanks, his walk up the slope to his millsite, the trouble that he had with the magneto, and the trip back home to get a different one. When he reached the Bagley property line, he told of seeing the warning sign, of getting out to read it, then his walk up the slope where he saw

126

Bagley stepping over a downed yucca barricade with his gun drawn. He said he turned to run back to his car to get his own rifle. It was then that Bagley fired and Keys returned the fire, aiming first at Bagley's gun hand.

"Bagley ran in an irregular manner—jumping as though he was trying to dodge the bullets—what we call gunman's tactics," Bill recalled.

"Did you see the gun in his hand as he was jumping and zigzagging?" D'Orr asked.

"Yes, sir. He was running sideways with the gun still in his hand."

"How many times did you shoot?"

"Well, as soon as I could catch up with him with my gun, I was holding it like this without taking sight," he said, standing up to demonstrate. "There was no time to sight. As soon as I caught up with him, I shot at him again. He turned to his left. Then I shot again immediately afterwards and he fell over out of sight. After that I couldn't see him."

Bill told of backing up and taking the long route home, having lunch there, and changing his clothes. When the defense attorney asked him to identify the clothes that he had worn that day, he pointed to the blue denim work trousers. Then he was shown the tan trousers on which the chemist had found blood stains. Bill said that he never wore them while working and that the blood stains had resulted from his frequent nose bleeds which happened any time during the night or day. He also stated that he had not gone anywhere near the body after the shooting.

Keys next related to the jury his return to the millsite, getting his pump to work again and filling his tank with about five hundred gallons of water for his stock. After this he drove down to about the same spot as earlier that morning, stopped the car but left the engine running. Here he looked around, then went a few feet beyond the warning sign. Again he saw no one. He decided to go no further because he "didn't know whether the man was dead or not and expected shooting." Shortly afterwards he went on into Twentynine Palms to turn himself in to Judge Poste.

After Bill's testimony had been completed, D'Orr made

127

an important point concerning Bill's defense. "Mr. Keys. From your previous meetings with Mr. Bagley, his appearance, the statements that he made to you, and the threats that were communicated to you throughout the history of his residence in that territory, did you believe that he was a man with a deranged mind?"

"Yes, sir. I did," Bill answered definitely.

"Did you believe him to be a dangerous man?"

"Yes, sir."

"And one more question. When you fired the lethal shots, did you believe then that your life was in imminent peril?"

"Yes, sir. I did."

At this point D'Orr once again attempted to have the statement of Bagley's doctors introduced into evidence concerning the deceased's mental state, but District Attorney Neblett objected loudly that they were hearsay and not relevant. After lengthy argument by the two counsels, Judge Freeman sustained the objection and the statements were not admitted into evidence.

When John Neblett took his place before Mr. Keys to begin his cross-examination, he started with questions about his early history in the desert area. Bill said that he had lived on the desert since 1898, that he had come to work at the Desert Queen Mine in 1910, and that his principal occupation was mining until 1918 when he also started to graze cattle. He also talked about the road that went through his property and the one passing through Bagley's. At one gate where the road passed into Bagley's place from the west were signs reading "Trespassing at your own risk" and "Grazing of cattle, $1.00 per head per day." He also told of driving his cattle regularly from 1936 until 1943 to and from Pleasant Valley except in 1943, when the gate was locked. After he had complained to the Land Office, the gate had been opened.

Then the questioning shifted to the fence around Bagley's property.

"Now, Mr. Keys, tell us about the fence that you built around Bagley's place."

"Well, Mr. Lawrence and his son, Bill, worked for me in 1938 and part of '39. We strung about 3,700 feet of fence around part of the Bagley property."

"What was the nature of that fence?"

"It was a two-strand, barbed wire fence. The wire was taken from my own fenceline which was already up, and one spool of new wire was taken from my ranch. We cut the posts near the Quail Springs Wash."

"Now, did Mr. Bagley furnish any wire for this project?"

"He did not," Bill said emphatically, "but we did buy some from him—part of a spool."

"And the expense of this fence was borne by you?"

"I didn't get that," Bill said, looking directly at the District Attorney.

Neblett repeated the question, more slowly this time. "The expense of constructing this fence was borne by you? In other words, you paid for it."

"Yes. That's right."

"Now, if I understand you correctly, Mr. Keys, that fence was built, according to your understanding, so that you would be permitted to use the road that went through Bagley's west gate and then on to his well, as well as from the well on north to your millsite. Is that correct?"

"Yes, sir. That was the understanding."

"Had you been using that road prior to that time?"

"I had. We were traveling that road right by his house previous to the fence. That was the main road then. There were many people milling ore at my mill. They always traveled that road up until the time that I made the fence."

Neblett considered Bill's replies for a few seconds before continuing. "Now Mr. Keys. At about the time you were building this fence, Mr. Bagley was making concrete blocks for his house, was he not?"

"Yes. He was using sand from the wash that crosses his road between the well and his house."

"Did Mr. Bagley ever communicate a complaint to you regarding your stock coming upon his property at night and stepping upon and breaking those concrete blocks?"

"Yes, he did. He complained to Mr. Lawrence."

129

"And how many head of stock were you grazing at that time?"

"Well, we had in the neighborhood of two hundred."

"Two hundred?" the District Attorney asked, as if to emphasize the number. "Was there any other fence in this area other than this one you built?"

"That's all."

"That is the only one between the pump and Mr. Bagley's property?"

"Yes—the only one."

"Now Mr. Keys, let's return to the Spanish Jack that you mentioned earlier. Did it ever turn up after you accused Mr. Bagley of killing it?"

"It did not. It couldn't have, because it was dead."

"And with respect to the cow that was killed, I understand that you took the bullet out of that cow and turned it over to the sheriff?"

"Yes, sir. I did."

Neblett walked over to his table and removed a piece of paper before returning to his witness a few seconds later. "Mr. Keys. Were you ever advised that the bullet together with a .22 rifle obtained from Mr. Bagley had been submitted to a ballistic expert in Los Angeles? Did you know that he expressed the opinion that the bullet was not from a .22 Winchester rifle, or a .22 Remington rifle, or from the rifle that Worth Bagley had submitted for examination?"

"No, I was never notified what became of that bullet after I turned it in."

Bill's answer seemed to surprise Neblett, who went on to a new subject. "Tell us when was the first time Bagley directly communicated any threat to you."

Bill thought for a few moments before answering. "That was when we were at the quarter post between my land and Bagley's sometime in 1937. We were trying to determine the line from that quarter post. Some boys were at the southeast corner of that section holding up a flag. I was sighting from this quarter post to the corner post when Bagley drove up. He was in his truck when he said, 'You don't need to run that line. I have run it and whatever I have established is the line.'

130

Well, I said, 'I would like to establish the line here and know just where it is when I build the fence.' Then the conversation came up about cattle. Bagley said, 'If your cattle come on my land, I'll shoot them the next time.' All of this time he was fingering his six-shooter which he had strapped on his side. He concluded our conversation with a couple more threats, saying, 'Don't try to run any line. Don't tell the Land Office I'm going to move a stake that is over north of here, or I will do you like the cattle.'"

"Now when you saw him fingering his six-shooter, were you in fear of bodily injury at that time?"

"Yes, I was," Bill answered. "I called to Mr. Murphy, who was a little over from us, and he hurried over."

"And how far was Bagley from you at the time?"

"About thirty feet."

"Where was your gun at that time?"

"I didn't have any."

"You had no gun?" Neblett asked in disbelief.

"No," came Bill's firm reply.

"Did you believe at that time that Mr. Bagley was going to shoot you?"

"I wasn't sure. He was mad, wild-eyed like a crazy person talking that way."

"Were you worried about Bagley threatening Murphy?"

"Yes, sir. We all stood at the quarter post when a woman came running down from Bagley's house to the road where we were. The woman we didn't know. There were no doors on the truck in which Bagley was seated so we could see that he also had a rifle in the cab with him. The rifle was sitting right by the steering post. Then the other boys who were helping me walked up and Bagley drove off."

Neblett kept Bill on the stand for another hour going over in detail the previous testimony that had been brought out by Paul D'Orr concerning Bagley's threats to him. By then it was after four o'clock so court was adjourned until the next morning. Bill was exhausted from his full day of testimony, compounded by the cold from which he was still suffering. After conferring with his attorneys and Frances, he was led back to his cell where he anticipated a good night's rest.

XVII

July 22, 1943
Thursday

When Bill awoke on the tenth day of his trial, he found that his previous night's sleep had done little to diminish his cold. After completing his regular morning exercises and his breakfast tray, he felt much better. He was more in control of his thoughts by the time he returned to the witness stand at ten o'clock. Then District Attorney John Neblett resumed his cross-examination, starting with a question that hadn't been previously discussed during the trial.

"Mr. Keys. When did you place that 'No Trespassing' sign on that Joshua tree near your property line and Bagley's?"

"In 1930, but it wasn't a 'No Trespassing' sign."

"Well, what did it say?"

"It said, 'Do not burn brush or destroy natural growths."

Once again Bill's answer seemed to take Neblett by surprise. "All right, we'll pass on to other things. At the time that you came by Mr. Bagley's well that morning, was he there?"

"No."

"You saw no one at that point, or had no conversation with anyone at that time?"

"No one."

"And then you drove on up that road to your well?"

"That's right. I pumped water into the large tank which ran by gravity into the two troughs."

"How long did you pump, Mr. Keys?"

"Oh, I judge I pumped a half hour or so."

"Were the troughs dry at the time you started pumping?"

"Not quite, but they were almost."

Bill was then questioned again about the succeeding events of changing the magneto, as well as his trip to the spot where he saw the sign in the middle of the road.

"I came to that county line. There was a sign five or six feet back from the line. I couldn't quite read it from the machine, so I backed up and got out and looked at the sign."

"Did you expect to see Mr. Bagley, as you walked up the rise?"

"No, not necessarily. I wanted to see what was in the road, and if it was possible to travel it or not."

"When you reached that point in the middle of the rise, what did you do?"

"I looked over the rise and saw a man moving. He was stepping over a large yucca that had been placed across the road."

"Did you at that time recognize Worth Bagley?"

"Yes, sir. I did."

"What did you do next?"

"I ran back to my machine and pulled my gun out. When he came up and fired, I let go and fired also."

"As far as this gun is concerned," Neblett said, lifting Bill's rifle from the exhibit table, "you must pull the trigger each time that you fire?"

"Each time."

Neblett put the gun back down onto the table, then turned back to his witness.

"Did you watch him from the time that he came over the log until he arrived at the top of the rise?"

"No, I didn't."

"All right, when did you lose sight of Mr. Bagley?"

"Just as soon as I turned to go back to the machine. The next time I saw him is when he came up on the rise."

The District Attorney walked back to the exhibit table, and this time picked up a different weapon. "Here's Bagley's revolver," he said, picking it up. Then he returned with it, handing it to Bill. "Please show us how he acted that day."

Bill took the weapon, got up from his seat, and walked

133

around the witness stand until he faced the District Attorney in front of the courtroom. Then he backed up about fifteen feet away. "Well, he came along like this," Bill said, demonstrating a stooped-over posture, "with his gun held at chest level. Then he fired and jumped to the left."

"He didn't extend his arm?" inquired Neblett.

"No. He kept it close to his body."

Bill demonstrated Bagley's motions of zigzagging after the first shot had struck him, turning him to the west.

"After you fired the third shot, show me how he fell."

Bill dropped to the floor with his hands out above his head, his right hand still clutching the revolver.

"He fell with his hands out?"

"Yes, sir," he said, getting up from the courtroom floor.

"He didn't buckle? He just went over?"

"Well, he might have taken one step before falling with his hands sprawled out."

"Thank you, Mr. Keys. You may resume your seat on the stand."

Neblett waited a few moments before continuing. "Now Mr. Keys, you were still in the same position that you were in at the Joshua tree and by your car when you fired the first shot?"

"Yes. I hadn't moved during the entire time."

"The three shots that you fired were all about equally spaced in time?"

"Yes, sir. There was a little time before I could catch up with him with my gun."

"Had anything been said by either of you prior to the shots being fired?"

"No. Nothing was said."

"And when you first saw him, you were unarmed?"

"When he came over to the yucca, I was unarmed."

"After you saw Mr. Bagley fall, what did you do?"

"I got into my machine, backed up about seventy-five feet or so until I found a spot to turn around, then headed back to my ranch, taking the long way."

"What did you do with your rifle?"

"I put it in the seat with me."

"Did you reload it at that time?"

"No. I reloaded it after I got home."

Neblett then took him once again through his activities of the afternoon until he turned himself in to Judge Poste.

"Now Mr. Keys, at the time you came to your well that morning were you in fear of bodily injury from Bagley?"

"Well, I was prepared for trouble," came Bill's immediate answer. "I thought that he might stop me on the road there."

"If he had stopped you, did you intend to use that gun?"

"Well, if he had stopped me on the road, the chances are he would have gotten me before I could have even gotten out of the car."

"Now as you walked up the road to the point from which you first saw Mr. Bagley, were you at that time in fear of bodily injury?"

"I knew there was going to be a shooting."

"When did you first know that?"

"When I first saw his gun in his hand."

"Were you in fear when you ran back to your car to get your gun?"

"Not exactly. I stood there with the gun in my hand thinking he might speak to me when I saw him approach."

"You made an effort to speak to him?"

"No."

"You didn't offer to leave the property?"

"No. I was on my own property," Bill answered.

"Well, the surveyor's map indicates that you're incorrect, does it not?"

Bill considered the question for a moment, remembering the map that had been presented on the first day of the proceedings. "Well, it might be. I was in between my car and the Joshua tree. That's what I took to be the property line."

"Now you stated to me in my office on the fourteenth of May that you wanted Bagley to fire the first shot. Is that correct?"

"That's correct. I didn't want to fire the first shot."

"And while you were waiting for him to fire first, were you in fear of bodily injury at his hands at that time?"

"Well, I might have been, but I wasn't what you might say

135

frightened or anything. I felt that I was capable of handling my gun."

"Have you ever been faced with a similar situation when a man pointed a gun at you and fired?"

"Yes," Bill answered. His thoughts immediately returned to 1930 when Homer Urton drew on him near his Desert Queen Mine. That young cowboy learned how fast Bill's draw was. Luckily he only had a bullet through his arm to show for his folly. In the trial that followed, the jury found Bill innocent. Bill's mind snapped back to the present, as Neblett went on with his questions.

"Now do you recall an occasion when you and Mr. Lawrence were working on the pump at your millsite, and Mr. Bagley drove up and Mr. Lawrence went over to speak to him?"

"Yes, I remember that day very clearly."

"Do you recall hearing any of the conversation that transpired between the two men?"

"No, I don't. I was too far away to hear what was said."

"At the time Mr. Lawrence was talking with Bagley who remained in his car, did you not go over to your own car to get your rifle and to place it over by the pump?"

"No, I don't believe I did. In fact, I don't recall taking the rifle out of the car at all," he said definitely, looking right at the District Attorney.

"Do you recall any conversation with Mr. Lawrence after Bagley had driven away?"

"Yes, I certainly do."

The District Attorney walked away from the defendant toward the jury before turning around from that point to speak.

"The witness has stated that at no time did he make any threats against Mr. Bagley. I will ask you, if at that time, after Mr. Bagley had departed and Mr. Lawrence returned to the pump, that you did not tell Mr. Lawrence that you at all times wanted your gun near you when Bagley was present, and that you would like to get him in the sights of your .30 calibre automatic? Did you make that statement?"

"No, sir. I never said anything like that," Bill answered flatly.

"The prosecution has no more questions. Your witness, Mr. D'Orr."

Paul D'Orr got up from his chair to exchange places with John Neblett.

"Mr. Keys, if Bagley had not come up on the rise, leveled his gun and fired at you, would you have shot him?"

"No, sir. I wouldn't have."

"Did you intend to kill or wound Bagley unless he attacked you under the threat of death or maiming?"

"I did not."

"If Bagley had come up on the rise and had spoken to you—"

"If he had spoken, I would not have fired at him," again he answered definitely.

"When you fired, did you believe that Bagley was shooting to kill you?"

"I had every reason to believe so."

"Now Mr. Keys, were you seeking trouble with Mr. Bagley on this day that you went to your mill?"

"I was not. I hadn't even seen him in a long time."

"So the fact is, you hadn't had any trouble with Mr. Bagley, hadn't talked with him for more than a year, perhaps going on two years?"

"That's right."

"Now Mr. Keys, when you stated to the District Attorney that before you shot, you desired him to shoot first, what did you mean by that?"

"Well, I didn't want to shoot first, as I thought he might speak to me. Instead of speaking, he shot, and then I shot after that."

"Then you never intended to shoot Mr. Bagley except in the event of saving your own life?" his attorney questioned.

"That's correct."

"Thank you, Mr. Keys. That's all the questions I have for you."

Bill got up and returned to his seat next to Tom Reynolds,

D'Orr's assistant. D'Orr called Mrs. Della Dudley as his next witness.

The white-haired lady from Chino moved quickly and unhesitantly to take her place on the witness stand. She and her husband, Howard, had retired from missionary service in Burma after more than twenty-five years. Despite being in her late sixties, she had as much energy now as when she first arrived at Bill's Desert Queen Ranch in 1937. She was the last of a series of teachers who taught at the Desert Queen School attended by Bill's children and those of neighboring homesteaders. She and Howard would remain five years, sharing their knowledge and experiences in shaping the minds of her young students. Through her guidance, class trips to Los Angeles were arranged and a student newspaper was published. Its articles and artwork reflected the influence of the desert on their lives. The school closed its doors for the last time in 1942 when the younger Keys children were old enough to attend high school in Alhambra, and there weren't enough other students to continue. Her excellence in teaching was not only reflected in her students' later lives, but also in the awards that she was given by a national teachers organization. She modestly accepted a monetary award of seventy-five dollars, only to donate it to the China Relief Fund in the name of her students.

While she was living and teaching at Bill's ranch, she was neighborly with just about everyone that she met, including Worth Bagley. Her testimony today revolved around a visit she had made to his ranch sometime in late 1940 or the spring of 1941.

"Now Mrs. Dudley, will you tell us what Worth Bagley said at the time of your visit to his ranch?" Paul D'Orr asked.

"Well, he said the police had been out there to see him, and that they had brought a letter written by Bill Keys to the Riverside County District Attorney. Bagley said, 'Bill Keys said I killed a cow of his, but I didn't kill his cow. I don't know anything about it.' Then he said, 'I'm not shooting his cows, but when I do shoot, I'll shoot Bill Keys.'"

138

"What was Mr. Bagley's appearance during this conversation?"

Della Dudley paused a moment to compose her words carefully before speaking.

"Well, we often met Mr. Bagley. As long as I knew him, I don't remember once when we talked about Mr. Keys that he wasn't excited, angry or rather wild. I personally considered him badly mentally balanced," she said.

"Mr. Neblett, you may cross-examine."

The District Attorney walked forward to the witness. "Now, Mrs. Dudley, when you had this discussion with Mr. Bagley, were you alone?"

"No, my husband was with me."

"You weren't afraid of Mr. Bagley, were you?"

"When I first knew him, I wasn't, Mr. Neblett. Afterwards, I wasn't afraid for myself, but I knew that he intended to kill Mr. Keys. I knew it for sure. I wouldn't ever want to make him angry at me."

"What was Mr. Keys' attitude toward Mr. Bagley?"

"Never in the five years in which I lived with Mr. Keys as one of his family, did he ever make one threat against Worth Bagley. That I swear to," she affirmed positively.

"Did Mr. Keys ever make threats against anybody else?"

"No. He never did."

"From the time that you lived at the Keys' ranch, did you become familiar with the reputation of Mr. Keys in that area for peace and quiet?"

Paul D'Orr immediately jumped up from his chair. "I object, your Honor! That question is incompetent and a breech of misconduct on the part of the District Attorney. The character of the defendant for peace and quiet is not an issue. Furthermore, it's an invasion of his Constitutional rights."

"I apologize and withdraw the question," Neblett said. "We have no further questions of this witness. Thank you."

"Nor does the defense," voiced D'Orr from his chair.

"The witness may be excused," Judge Freeman said, adding, "It's late and time that we break for our lunch recess. The jury is reminded as before."

Later that afternoon the District Attorney called Deputy C. F. McCracken back to the stand to testify in rebuttal.

"Now, Mr. McCracken. At the time that you visited the scene of the shooting, and Mr. Keys designated certain points to you, did he describe to you the manner in which Worth Bagley fired at him?"

"He did. Yes, sir."

"Please show us how he demonstrated to you at that time," Neblett said, handing the lawman Bagley's revolver that he had just picked up from the exhibit table.

"Well, he held his arm straight out like this," he said, demonstrating. "Mr. Keys said his arm was straight out."

"Then he did not demonstrate his position as being chest level?"

"No, sir. He didn't," came the lawman's reply.

"Counsel, you may cross-examine," Neblett offered.

"Now, Mr. McCracken, when he showed you, he extended his arm a little further than he extended it this morning when he was demonstrating to the District Attorney?" questioned Paul D'Orr, in an attempt to reverse the effect of this witness's testimony.

"Yes, he extended his arm out straight—both on the evening of May 11th and early in the afternoon on May 12th."

"Now you are a sharpshooter. From about 104 feet away with an assailant firing at you, would you be able to tell in that fraction of time just how far out a man had held his arm extended?"

McCracken thought for a few seconds before answering. "I could not answer that question," he said bluntly.

"And wouldn't it be much harder to tell how far a man had his arm extended if you were in front of him on a line, rather than on the side of him looking at his arm laterally?"

Again the witness paused a minute to visualize the question. "I would say yes."

"That's all the questions that we have," announced D'Orr.

"Thank you, Mr. McCracken. That's all. We rest, your Honor," voiced the District Attorney.

And court then went into recess.

XVIII

July 23, 1943
Friday

Word passed like electricity among those standing in the hallway that the jury had finally reached a verdict after five hours of deliberation. The spectators quickly rejoined the others who already were seated in Riverside Superior Court #1. Among those waiting with Frances Keys and her children were a number of their close friends including Daisy Kiler, Della Dudley and the Perkinses. They were as anxious as everyone else in the room to hear what fate the jury had decided for Bill.

Earlier that morning they had listened as District Attorney John Neblett gave his closing argument for the prosecution on this eleventh and last day of the trial. He had flatly stated that Bill Keys was guilty of murder in the first degree. He emphasized Ray Pinker's theory that Worth Bagley had been on the ground at the time he was shot. He had further emphasized for the jury that the defendant was trespassing when he walked beyond the warning sign on the Bagley property. Bill had made no effort to retreat even after he had seen Bagley approach with a gun in his hand.

Neblett had also pointed out that Bagley's tracks indicated that his back was towards Keys, that he was undoubtedly seeking cover—even running away from him.

"Could that be a question of self-defense?" he asked.

In an effort to substantiate his argument, he questioned Keys' reputation as a man of peace. "Why weren't witnesses called on his behalf?" he had asked. Even Mrs. Dudley, who had been a friend for five years, had not been questioned on his reputation for peace and quiet in his neighborhood. Neblett had added that "the record is silent in that respect, and that silent witness speaks more loudly and eloquently than anyone with respect to the character of William F. Keys."

In equally eloquent fashion he had tried to cast a shadow of doubt on the truth of Bill's testimony. Many in the courtroom still remembered his words which had certainly had their effect on the jury. He had said with fervor, "It is obvious that Bill Keys had endeavored to withhold from you the entire truth which is within his knowledge and his knowledge alone. No other man knows the whole truth as to what actually occurred that morning in the desert."

Now the jury was returning to their seats to reveal to the court how convincing the prosecution's argument had been. Hardly a sound could be heard in the room as Judge Freeman spoke. "Has the jury reached a verdict?"

"We have, your Honor," said the jury foreman, standing up and handing a slip of paper to the bailiff. It was passed to the judge, who adjusted his glasses before opening the paper.

After glancing at what was written, he looked up to the waiting room. "Will the defendant rise?" he commanded. Bill and his attorneys stood in unison to hear the verdict delivered by the foreman. "How do you find the defendant?"

"Your Honor. We find the defendant, William F. Keys, guilty of manslaughter."

Bill's face mirrored the shock and disbelief that he felt as the word "guilty" impressed itself firmly in his mind. These same feelings were seen in the faces of his family and friends as they sat numb and silent. "There must be some mistake," Bill thought to himself. "The evidence was plain. I told the truth. How could I be guilty? It was a pure case of self-defense." He barely heard his attorney make the motion for a new trial. Nor did he hear the judge reply that he would make a decision on that motion when they met the following Tuesday at ten o'clock for sentencing. After the judge's gavel sounded and the courtroom started to clear, Bill sat down to begin to realize the gravity of his situation.

XIX

August 4, 1943
Wednesday

Bill Keys had returned to Judge Freeman's court on July 27th as ordered to hear his sentence pronounced for manslaughter. There had been few spectators in the courtroom that Tuesday morning. Frances was there, as she had been every day of her husband's three-week trial. This day she was also joined by her four children. Patricia and Phyllis, her youngest daughters, sat with Willis and Virginia, her two oldest, who had taken the day off from their jobs in a Los Angeles defense plant. Despite the court's verdict, the Keys family stood in support of their husband and father.

While Bill's family was present, his attorneys were conspicuously absent. In their place they had filed a written motion with the court clerk for a new trial on the following grounds to be argued on August 3rd:

First—That the court erred upon the decisions of law arising during the course of the trial.

Second—That the court misdirected the jury in matters of law.

Third—That the verdict is contrary to law.

Fourth—That the verdict is contrary to evidence.

Fifth—That the district attorney was guilty of prejudicial misconduct during the course of the trial in the presence of the jury.

Now one week later Judge Freeman heard Paul D'Orr's and Thomas Reynolds' arguments. District Attorney John Neblett replied to D'Orr's argument that there was no evidence of hostility on the part of Keys by recalling Bill's own testimony from the trial transcript. Bill had stated that upon seeing Bagley, he ran to his car and took out his rifle "prepared for trouble."

Judge Freeman's decision was not unexpected. He denied the motion for a new trial and sentenced Bill Keys to San Quentin prison for a period of one to ten years. His attorneys immediately gave oral notice of appeal. As a result, they and the District Attorney adjourned to the judge's chambers. There they discussed the bail which could be set for Bill's release pending the ruling of the appeals court. The court fixed bail at $10,000.

That had been yesterday. Today while Bill was back in his cell at the Riverside jail, he had been visited by several reporters. He spoke of his mines, his family, his ranch, and his hopes for the future. Part of his interview appeared in the day's *Riverside Daily Press:*

"I expect to be back on my 800 acre ranch within a few days. Mrs. Keys and friends are working to secure bondsmen. There are two men, one in Ontario and one in Los Angeles, who have signified their willingness to go on the bond. I will need the signatures of two Riverside County residents to the bond, however. Then I will go back to my desert property to await the ruling of the appellate court to which an appeal from the judgment of the superior court on a motion for a new trial has been made."

Prison,
Parole,
And
Pardon

XX

March 24, 1944
Friday

The cellblock at the Riverside jail changed occupants daily. Some remained there only a day or two. Others were held overnight until they made bail. Still others stayed for months. Their faces became as familiar as the cracks in the cell walls when they met outside in the yard during the exercise period. Bill became one of these regulars who remained seven months after his sentencing. Here he waited the results of his appeal. Despite several attempts, Paul D'Orr had been unable to get his bail reduced. Bill's family had been equally unsuccessful in raising the full $10,000.

Except for visits from his family, lawyers, and a few close friends, his daily routine of eating, exercising, reading, and waiting was one that continued with little variation as the weeks dragged into months. There had been little reason for celebration in September, when his and Frances' birthdays occurred just three days apart. Except for a card from his family, the day slipped by without notice.

Despite his present confinement, Bill's mind was still as well-tuned as his body, and few things that occurred in his present surroundings missed his attention. Many years of prospecting had conditioned his attentive powers. As he traveled for weeks at a time through isolated desert areas, his very life had depended upon his ability to recognize landmarks and to remember where springs and waterholes were located. Like the Indians who had traveled there before him, he knew which plants could be eaten, which ones could be used as medicines, and which ones could kill him. Long ago he had learned from them how to grind mesquite beans into meal. This was then fermented to improve the taste. He also knew if he cut his hand, that the beavertail cactus could be pounded into a wet dressing to deaden the pain, as well as to promote healing.

Even back at the Desert Queen Ranch, his home remedies had often saved the lives of his cattle from leg infections. Often he or Frances had wrapped the wound with fresh cow manure to draw out the poison. Living as he had done in such isolation had afforded him with as valuable an education as that provided by any school. Now he broadened his education by spending some of his confinement time catching up on his reading—a luxury that his long work days at the ranch had left him little time to do.

For five months his cellmate had been an eighteen-year-old youth sentenced for vagrancy, but the differences in their ages seemed to be no barrier between them. Like the other inmates with whom he came in contact, they got along well. In time they hated the burnt rice and carrot soup that frequently showed up on their meal trays. After being spoiled by many years of Frances' good cooking, he found that the prison food did not help to build his morale.

The frustraton of confinement, as well as his inability to get his bail reduced or the necessary money raised, caused his morale to drop even lower. As a result of his own trial, he began to wonder whether or not California justice was a myth. The more time he spent thinking about the whole Bagley affair, the more he convinced himself that it had been a set-up. He was sure that his fate had finally been sealed by the influential cattle family with whom he had had so much trouble in the past.

After he had homesteaded part of their range, his fences blocked its use by their cattle. There had been years of harassment. His fences had been cut. Some of his cattle had disappeared or turned up with those of the cattle company at roundup time. When old buildings located a half mile from his ranch house were dismantled and stolen from his property, he took the cattlemen to court. After months of waiting for his five hundred dollar judgment from them, he returned to San Bernardino to discover that the court's verdict had never been officially entered on record. The buildings were a total loss for him.

Then there had been the Homer Urton shooting, and finally the developing feud with Bagley. Now since he had been in jail, the National Park Service had given his pending grazing permit to Jim Stocker, the Undersheriff who had taken over when the large cattle company moved their operation to the mountains near Big Bear. Perhaps Bagley's hatred of him had been influenced by these cattlemen in hopes of getting rid of him forever. These charges he could not prove. But he felt strongly that there was more than just a chance coincidence here, and Frances felt the same way.

After the trial had concluded, Frances returned to her job at a Los Angeles defense plant. Despite her full-time work and her inability to drive, she still managed to visit her husband. When family or friends couldn't bring her, she rode the bus from Alhambra, a practice begun when Daisy wasn't able to come to the trial.

Even on the days when she went to Riverside, she still managed to care for the needs of her four children. At night after she had washed the dishes and the children were either asleep or doing their school lessons, her day was far from over. She could usually be found sitting at the kitchen table typing letters or taking care of the family's business affairs. After her marriage to Bill, he had gladly allowed her to take charge of the ranch's financial records, as well as to answer most of their correspondence. In the last few months her brother Aaron had moved out to look after their property, but she knew that this could only be temporary. He had his own family responsibilities in Huntington Beach. Therefore in October she and Bill had decided to sell their sixty-one head of cattle to help to pay Bill's legal expenses. This also alleviated the need for a full-time person to live at their ranch.

Since the trial, dozens of letters had passed through her typewriter. In them, she told their friends of Bill's predicament and hoped they might be able to help raise the money for his bail. Soon her hopes were raised when close friends agreed to loan them the necessary amount so that Bill could be home with his family for Christmas. Their hopes were just as suddenly dashed when their benefactor needed the intended funds for a serious operation and withdrew the offer.

Frances was heartbroken when she received this news. She was physically tired and the strain of the last seven months had had a marked effect on her health. Her light brown hair was turning white. A recent bout with flu after Thanksgiving had further reduced her strength, as well as her spirits. So it was no surprise that with Bill remaining in jail, she and the rest of the family had decided against a big Christmas dinner or celebration this year.

Yet Frances was not a quitter. She refused to give up. She continued to work on her husband's behalf, writing two letters to the judges of the Court of Appeals when she learned that they were about to make their decision on his trial. In these long typewritten letters she carefully outlined the history of their troubles with the cattlemen, pointing an accusing finger not only at them, but also toward certain members of the Riverside and San Bernardino County Sheriff's Offices, whom she felt were in league with them. After she mailed the letters she waited, hopeful that further investigations would be made by this higher court. Perhaps justice would finally be served, righting the wrongs that her Bill had suffered.

Five weeks later on February fifteenth, Paul D'Orr received word at his Los Angeles office that the District Court of Appeals had reached a decision. That same day he had a copy of their fifteen-page brief in his hands which outlined the Bagley-Keys conflict and then discussed the serious errors that they found had been made in Bill Keys' trial.

The denial of Bagley's medical records as evidence detailing his brain tumor and history of his erratic behavior was found to be the first error. Other errors were found in several instructions that Judge Freeman had given to the jury just prior to their withdraw for deliberation. In one

150

instruction Freeman had singled out the defendant as the only witness to the shooting and had cast doubt on the credibility of his testimony. This they deemed to be unfair.

The court judge in three other instructions to the jury had inferred that Bill had created the situation of putting himself in immediate peril of death or of bodily harm by trespassing. As a result he was not eligible for full protection from the law. The higher court said that there was not sufficient evidence to prove this, and it was therefore viewed as another court error.

D'Orr read slowly the last part of their decision. "As there were serious errors in the instructions, we must consider the question of whether or not those errors resulted in a miscarriage of justice. In approaching this question, we are impressed with the statements of the defendant who when testifying tried to minimize the damaging effect of his admission to the officers on the day of the killing by saying that the deceased was jumping sideways to make himself a difficult target. This does not alter the established facts that the deceased was killed by a shot in the back and that markings on the ground indicated that he was running away when the fatal shot was fired."

"The law of self-defense is based on reasonable appearance of imminent peril of death or of serious bodily injury to the party assailed. Thus with the above evidence, we fail to understand how any intelligent jury could have found the defendant not guilty. Certainly the facts establish that Bagley had abandoned the conflict and was running away when the defendant killed him. Thus, danger to the defendant was not imminent, and under the law of self-defense, he had no right to take Bagley's life. In view of these facts which were clearly placed before the jury, it does not seem reasonable to suppose that the erroneous instructions could have led that body into error when the evidence, including the statements of the defendant himself, showed his guilt and that he had no right to kill when he did under the law of self-defense. We therefore conclude that there has been no miscarriage of justice in this case and that the judgment and prison sentence are affirmed."

Paul D'Orr finished reading the higher court's ruling, then read the entire document again. Later that day he drove to Riverside personally to break the news to his client. With its delivery Bill's months of waiting were over. Five weeks later, during the week of March 24th, he was transported to San Quentin where he began serving his sentence for manslaughter.

XXI

The Prison Years
1944-1948

Bill's concern for his ranch property was as great as his determination to prove his own innocence. Having arrived in that desert canyon over thirty years ago with almost nothing, he had worked long and hard to make it and the resulting Desert Queen Ranch a fine home for himself and his family. He may have temporarily lost his freedom, but he wasn't going to lose his ranch too.

In one of their last visits together before his transfer to San Quentin, he and Frances had decided their place had been vacant too long, and that she and the younger girls should move back to the desert as soon as school ended in a few months. Pat and Phyllis could start school in Twenty-nine Palms the following fall. On June first, Willis drove his mother and sisters home, then returned to Alhambra to make two more trips in a rented stake-bed truck to move their furniture and belongings. He and Virginia would temporarily remain at their jobs in Los Angeles.

The returning family discovered what they already knew, that living in the desert is a full-time job demanding not only time but boundless energy. In their two-year absence the effects of sun, wind, and rain were obvious. The adobe walls of their barn had started to crumble and its wooden roof was missing shakes. Four-foot high saltbushes, brush, and other weeds now grew in the yard, in the orchard, and in the empty corrals. All of this would have to be cut, for as the heat of summer progressed, the brush would become tinder dry—a

153

potential fire danger to the safety of their ranch. Their pear and other fruit trees needed pruning, the hard packed soil under them cleared of weeds and loosened, the garden replanted, and the irrigation system activated again. Even the house needed repairs and thorough cleaning. Their first day would be spent sweeping away the evidence of visiting packrats who had made it their home during the Keys' absence.

The whole family went to work once again. They worked side by side, with Frances directing their efforts as they went from one project to another. Even her brother, Aaron Lawton, returned to help with the heavier work, staying a week at a time. Al and Buster, her other brothers, alternated their visits with Aaron, to provide a man at the ranch as often as possible in Bill's absence. Over the summer their teamwork began to show its effect. The ranch in the rocky canyon slowly began to regain something of its former condition.

Soon the months slipped by. After the first frost, the cottonwoods along the wash behind the house turned to gold. Like the trees in the orchard, they soon would be stripped bare of their leaves by desert winds. The tiny quail who had hatched the previous spring were now as large as their parents whom they had followed since birth through the underbrush and under the rock boulders in search of food.

The arrival of cool weather had made outside work pleasanter but no easier. Chores still had to be done each morning before the younger girls went down to Twentynine Palms to attend high school, where Pat had started her senior year. Frances kept busy at home during the day, fixing meals for her brothers when they were there, as well as doing the laundry, sewing and cleaning chores that she had been doing for years.

In September Virginia's name appeared in the local *Desert Trail* newspaper when she became the first woman from the Twentynine Palms area to enlist in military service. Pharmacist's Mate Third Class Keys returned to the desert in November to visit her family from her assignment at the

U.S. Naval Hospital in Oceanside. In the next few months she would receive further training in laboratory techniques at Bethesda, Maryland, and then be transferred to the U.S. Naval Air Station at Traverse City, Michigan. Here she had the distinction of being one of only two Waves assigned to the base. She spent much of her duty time waiting in a base ambulance at the side of the airfield for possible accidents or landing mishaps.

About the same time that Virginia enlisted, her brother Willis changed jobs. He left his defense plant work to accept another job which offered better opportunities but not an automatic draft deferment. This resulted in his being drafted into the Army the following year. After basic training, he was shipped overseas into the Pacific. Prior to his induction he had ridden his motorcycle on the long trip up to San Quentin to see his dad. Bill had been in good spirits during their short visit, and the two men talked about the rest of the family, as well as the happenings back at the ranch.

Throughout his life Bill had always tried to make the most of each day. That habit was one that was hard to break even with his present confinement in prison. Instead of changing his lifestyle, he merely adapted it to his new surroundings. Years later he would refer to this period of his life as his education, for he spent his free time reading, catching up on current affairs, and tackling new subjects for which he had never had time previously.

One of these interests was calligraphy. Hour after hour he practiced using his ink pen to create the elaborate style letters. He perfected his technique, mastering a number of script styles, before learning to use an air brush to put them onto paper. Combining these new skills with his ability to create poetry, he designed beautiful cards for members of his family at holiday times. Frances, the children, and many of their friends who received these original works of art from Bill saved them.

His artistic ability also revealed itself in the watercolor paintings that he created—paintings whose subjects were almost always outdoor scenes. He had a good eye for perspective, as well as for detail. Many of the scenes that he

155

depicted were based on places that he had seen on his prospecting trips to the High Sierras in the early 1900's.

Mastering the guitar and working with leather were among his other interests. Although he had often been required by necessity to mend the harness and tack for his horses and mules, he now switched his efforts into making wallets and belts.

So the time passed for Bill. He spent another Christmas away from his family and the desert that he loved. In March 1946 he made application for a full pardon to the California Adult Authority. They reviewed his prison record, and although he had been a model prisoner, they turned him down. They were considering him for a parole, but this offer Bill refused. In his mind, to accept parole would be to admit that he had been guilty in the first place. He was willing to complete his entire sentence if necessary until he could prove his innocence.

Frances, too, had faith in her husband and still believed in his innocence. Earlier she had ridden a bus to Sacramento to see Governor Earl Warren, but her appointment with him had accomplished nothing for Bill. Several times she had gone to San Quentin to see him, and after each visit they both felt better.

She lived on the hope of his eventual return, as she waited back at the ranch. By 1947 her vigil became a solitary one at times, as Pat had married and moved nearby to Joshua Tree. Many nights after she had finished her day's chores and Phyllis had gone to bed, Frances went into the living room to sit in her chair in front of the fireplace that Bill had built so long ago. The native granite was beautifully cut and fitted together, and on cold winter nights its warmth drifted through the entire house. Here she sat remembering the many happy years that they had been together. It was at such times that she often got out Bill's letters to reread them by the light from the kerosene lamp on the table. The lone light coming from the house was a silent reminder to anyone coming into the yard that Frances was still home waiting.

In the spring of 1948 her waiting and letter-writing paid off. From a friend she learned the whereabouts of Worth

156

Bagley's ex-wife, a potential defense witness whom they had hoped to call at Bill's trial, but whom they couldn't locate. Now Frances discovered that she had been living all of this time in the east Los Angeles area called Eagle Rock.

Frances went down to see her. After their talk, she was convinced that with her assistance Bill's innocence could be proven. But she would need expert legal help. Paul D'Orr, Bill's former attorney, had given up his regular law practice to work for a large company. Besides, the family wasn't able financially to hire another lawyer. They still owed D'Orr for his prior legal assistance. Willis and Viriginia's monthly allotments to their mother were the only income that she had. Then when she was at a loss as to where to turn, Frances thought of an old family friend and sat down to write a long letter to Erle Stanley Gardner.

*   *   *   *   *

Bill had met Gardner for the first time in 1927. The then lawyer liked to get away from his practice on the coast and to spend a few days relaxing by camping and writing out in the desert near the Keys ranch. After their chance meeting, Bill had invited Gardner to return with him to meet his family and to have dinner with them.

Gardner's half ton truck which had been custom-fitted with a little house on the back was a forerunner of today's self-contained camper. Frances remembered how impressed six-year-old Willis had been when he looked inside and saw how well equipped it was. It even had a bathtub! On another trip Gardner showed Willis and his parents a new steel bow he had just gotten. He was quite an archer, and when he released an arrow it flew high into the cloudless blue sky, landing moments later near the corral. This was one of the many visits Gardner made during the following years that Willis would always remember.

As the Keys family grew, Gardner gave up his law practice to devote his full-time attention to writing. Sometimes he turned out four Perry Mason mysteries a year besides writing numerous short articles and travel books on his trips

157

to the desert. His interest in this field had also shifted to include the Baja area, and in the intervening years he spent most of his vacations there rather than in the Twentynine Palms area.

Gardner's life was to change once again in 1946 when a three-part article about him in *The Saturday Evening Post* mentioned his early law career and how he had been a champion to the underdog. As a result, he and the magazine were deluged with letters concerning people who needed legal help. One case in particular interested him. It concerned a man who had been sentenced to the gas chambber for a rape-murder. The man's lawyer believed him innocent despite the court's affirmation and sent Gardner a copy of the court transcript. The former attorney read it and discovered that the evidence in it not only proved the man innocent, but also suggested the real criminal. A closer reading further indicated that it would have been necessary for the man to have been in two places at the same time in order to have committed the crime. As a result of Gardner's letter to a State Supreme Court Justice, the death sentence was commuted to life imprisonment until a full investigation was completed. The convicted man was later found innocent.

In 1948 Gardner was in New York City visiting an old friend, Harry Steeger, publisher of *Argosy* magazine. He mentioned to Erle that he wanted to change the magazine's format to something totally different. Erle suggested that so far no magazine had ever done anything to improve the administration of justice. In the course of their discussion, Gardner outlined his idea for a "Court of Last Resort," a forum where public sentiment would be the highest authority.

Gardner agreed to write the case histories, and Steeger would publish those of potentially innocent men whom Gardner felt had been wrongly convicted. After Gardner had presented the facts of the case, he would leave it up to *Argosy*'s readers to decide whether further investigations should be undertaken. If so, the case would be turned over to a panel of experts who were willing to donate their time

158

and experience in the interest of justice. For this work Gardner chose Dr. LeMoyne Snyder, an expert in forensic medicine who was also an attorney; Detective Raymond Schindler; Alex Gregory, an outstanding authority in the use of the polygraph; and Clark Sellers, an internationally known handwriting expert, as the main members of his court.

*   *   *   *   *

Frances Keys' appeal for help took Erle Stanley Gardner by surprise. It had been several years since he had last seen his desert friends, and he had been unaware of Bill's legal problems. After reading her lengthy letter which detailed the whole history of her husband's case, Gardner drafted a short reply to her indicating his willingness to look into the matter further.

The first few days were full ones for him, as he put everything aside to begin work on Frances' request. By the beginning of the following week, after he had located, read, and thoroughly digested the more than a thousand pages of trial transcripts, he too suspected that Bill's guilt was in serious doubt. But before acting on his own instincts, he decided to present the facts of the Keys case to *Argosy*'s readers for their verdict. The article in the June issue entitled "Cooking with Dynamite" resulted in a flood of letters requesting that his Court of Last Resort undertake a full investigation. As a result, Gardner and his team of experts went into action.

They studied thoroughly the court testimony, exhibits, maps, and photographs of the shooting site, and with Frances Keys as their guide, they came out to the desert to see where the actual shooting took place. While they were there, she gave them a firsthand account of life with their former neighbor, Worth Bagley.

On their return to the city, one of Gardner's associates, Dr. LeMoyne Snyder, was particularly interested in going over the reports and photographs of the Bagley autopsy. His careful reexamination of the photographs revealed to his trained eye that the fatal wound was actually located in the exact middle of the deceased's side rather than in his back as the prosecution had emphasized during the entire court proceedings. The doctor wondered how such a misinterpretation of the evidence could have been made when the photographs plainly showed the actual location.

Snyder's findings also indicated that Bagley had probably been zigzagging or using his police tactics at the moment that Bill fired the fatal shot, just as Bill had repeatedly told the arresting officers and the jury. If Bagley had been running away, the wound would have indeed been in his back and not in his side. This one point had been the deciding one on which the Appellate Court had denied Bill a new trial.

District Attorney Neblett's medical experts testified that the pear-shaped drops of blood on the desert vegetation indicated that Bagley had been shot while on the ground. But as Dr. Snyder dug deeper into these medical records, he discovered other evidence which cast doubt on the prosecution's theory. As the fatal bullet entered the deceased's body, it not only passed through a number of vital organs but also severed the abdominal aorta. Snyder's findings concluded that this severing would have caused his blood pressure to drop to zero. Thus there would not have been any blood flow at all. He reasoned that the pear-shaped stains were caused by Bagley's erratic movements—his fast moving body pitching forward immediately after the moment of bullet impact.

Other members of Gardner's team probed deeper, gathering the medical records that the court had not allowed Bill's attorneys to draw upon. More background information on Worth Bagley was discovered. The results of this all-out probe attracted the attention of California Assemblyman Vernon Kilpatrick, who was then also the chairman of a legislative committee on jails. He quickly offered his assistance, joining the other members of the Court with their investigation. It wasn't long before he too was convinced that Bill Keys had suffered wrongly at the hands of the justice system.

Through Kilpatrick's assistance, Gardner learned that at one time Bagley had killed one of his favorite dogs for no apparent reason in a fit of anger. Afterwards he had consulted a psychiatrist. Further study of his retirement physicals and his own request for that retirement, indicated that Bagley suffered from a brain tumor. He also located the divorce papers of Bagley's former wife, Isabelle Clark, who stated at the time of her suit that her husband intended to kill Bill Keys and had spent considerable time planning his execution. He thought it strange that no one had paid any attention to this forewarning.

Kilpatrick continued to put in long hours in his investigation. When he learned that Frances Keys had located Isabelle Clark, he got her address and contacted her in an attempt to have her sign a deposition about her life with her former husband. After several telephone conversations, he was finally able to convince her of the importance and need for her statement. She agreed to help her former neighbor, Bill Keys.

161

XXII

July 19, 1948
Monday

The car passed slowly along the 5300 block of Dahlia Drive, its two occupants watching the house numbers until they found the one that they were seeking. After parking out front, the middle-aged man and his young assistant, who was carrying a leather briefcase in one hand and a portable typewriter in the other, walked together towards the small stucco house. The house was similar to many others in this section of Eagle Rock. Inside an elderly woman watched their arrival through the half-opened curtains, then went to the front door to greet them.

"Miss Clark?" the man asked politely.

"No, I'm her mother," came the lady's reply.

"I'm California State Assemblyman Vernon Kilpatrick and this is my assistant."

"Please come in."

Mrs. Clark led her guests into the living room where her daughter was seated on the couch. She then left the room. Because of Isabelle's health, Kilpatrick had agreed to come personally to her home rather than put her through the inconvenience of coming to his office in Los Angeles. After his assistant set up her typewriter, he seated himself, adjusted his glasses, and began his questioning.

"Let's begin with your marriage to Worth Bagley," he said while his assistant began transcribing the conversation.

"Well," she began, "we married in January 1940 in Yuma, Arizona."

"And as far as you know at this time, you were his ninth wife?"

"I didn't know it at that time, but now I do. Yes, I was his ninth wife, and I think his last legal one."

"Had you been informed of any of his previous marriages at the time that you married him?" he asked, settling back into the chair.

"No, I was perfectly innocent of all of them. I guess everybody else knew it but me. I was aware that he had been married before. He told me that. But I never knew that he had all of these other previous marriages—not until he served papers on me for divorce. Even that was a surprise, as I didn't have any idea that he was going to do that."

"When did he serve those papers?"

"Well, he asked me to go to Banning with him one day from the ranch. We never had any fusses or fights like married people usually have. As we were walking along the street there, a woman came up to me and asked, 'Are you Mrs. Worth Bagley?' I said, 'Yes.' Then she handed me these papers. I was flabbergasted when I looked and saw what they were. I turned to Worth and said, 'What is this?' He answered, 'Well, read them.' So I took the papers and walked back to the car. When I got in to read the papers, I saw where he was filing for a divorce. That was the first I knew about it."

"When was that divorce completed? Did he get a divorce from you or you from him?" asked the Assemblyman.

"Well, I don't know how it worked out. He wanted an annulment, but I wouldn't stand for that."

"And at the time of the incident which causes us to be seeking this information, that is the gun duel between Mr. Keys and Mr. Bagley which resulted in the death of your ex-husband, was your divorce complete? Had the year elapsed?"

"Yes, the year had elapsed."

"Do you know whether he was married during the intervening time?"

"Well, he wasn't married, but he was living with a woman out at the ranch."

"Now Miss Clark, how did you happen to meet Worth Bagley in the first place?"

"Well, I met him through my sister. He used to come up to her place in Yucca Valley where she lived at the time. He would come up there uninvited, as she didn't even like him."

"Did you go out to the desert for your health?"

"Yes. I lived out there in Yucca Valley for three years."

"And how long did you know Mr. Bagley before you got married?"

"About a month, I should say. I wanted to wait awhile and not get married right away. I also wanted my mother with me when I got married, but he wouldn't stand for it. He wanted to be married immediately," she said, also settling back on her couch into a more relaxed position.

"Then shortly after you married Mr. Bagley, did you begin to get suspicious that there was something wrong about his intentions and his conduct as applied to yourself and to others?"

"Yes, that's right. The day after we were married Mr. Monstead, who lived over on an adjoining ranch, came over to our place early in the morning. When he came over, Worth wouldn't let him into the house, but met him out there by one of the trees where they talked. He never would tell me what their conversation was about. I suppose it was in regard to his marriage to me instead of to Monstead's sister who had been living with him. He didn't want me to know anything about it, but from this time on, things kept coming up that made me suspicious. I foolishly thought that I could still help him. I thought that he wasn't well, and I could help him some. I knew that I had to stay in the desert a few years yet to recover my own health. It was a foolish idea on my part. He didn't want to be helped," Miss Clark concluded.

"How long did you actually live with Worth Bagley?"

"Just about a year."

"And during that year's time, did you ever have any sense of fear?" he asked.

"Yes, I did. He didn't make a move unless he had a gun with him. Most of our trouble was over Mr. Keys, because I couldn't hate him or his wife. They had never done anything to me and seemed like such nice neighbors who just wanted to be left alone. Mrs. Keys had invited me over to their place, but Worth wanted me to hate them as he did. That was our only trouble."

"Can you tell me of any incidents which showed animosity on the part of Mr. Bagley toward Mr. Keys?"

The middle-aged woman paused for a moment to collect her thoughts before beginning.

"Yes, one day he had his long range rifle. It's like the ones they use in the Army. He was an ex-serviceman who had served in the Navy. Worth was shooting up on the hill where there was a large bush. The wind was blowing, as it usually does out there, and I asked him what he was shooting at. He said, 'I thought it was that old goat up there.' That's what he called Mr. Keys. Well, of course I was dumbfounded to hear a man make a statement like that."

"How long after you were married did this happen?"

"Oh, several months."

"Now tell about the incident of the shooting of Mr. Keys' burro."

"Well, two deputies from San Bernardino came out there to investigate the shooting of this burro which took place before we were married. When they got out there, they wanted Worth's rifle. Well, Worth went into the house and came out with my rifle, which he gave to them. They took it in to make a ballistic report on it. The deputies were entirely innocent, as they didn't know that it wasn't Worth's rifle. In fact, I didn't know that they had taken it until after they had gone. Then I missed it and asked him about it. Worth told me that he had given it to them. When I asked him what for, he said that they wanted to make a ballistic report on it in regards to the shooting of a burro. And when I asked him, 'Why did they take mine instead of yours?' he answered, 'It's all taken care of—just don't talk about it any more.'"

"And when instead he had another rifle with a much larger bore—a high powered one," added Kilpatrick.

"That's right. He had a collection of guns with several different kinds there."

"He didn't tell the officers that, did he?"

"No."

"What did the officers finally do with your rifle?"

"Well, they took it into Riverside, and it was several weeks before they brought it back again. I didn't know whether to say anything to them or not. I didn't at the time, but later I told Mr. Hair, one of the deputies, about it. He was a very good friend of mine."

"What was done with the bullet?"

"Mr. Keys had that. He had gotten it out of his dead burro, and he gave it to Mr. Hair, I believe, although I'm not sure about that," she said.

"Then there was the shooting of some of Mr. Keys' stock. Was there an incident of that kind that you remember?"

"Well, there were several of them, but I wasn't out there at the time that they happened."

"Are there any other instances of conflict between Mr. Bagley and Mr. Keys that occurred during the time that you were there?"

Isabelle Clark once again paused before answering.

"Well, no. Just as I told you, Mr. Bagley used to lie in wait for Mr. Keys just to catch him alone. He often told me, 'If I ever catch him alone without witnesses, I'll get rid of the old goat.'"

"What do you mean by 'lie in wait'? Did he hide on the roadside?" inquired Kilpatrick.

"Yes, beside the road. There's a wash on the ranch where he used to wait for Mr. Keys to come along. If I were out there, I could show you just where it was. I used to have to walk down there to get him for lunch."

"Was he armed?"

"Yes. He had his .38 with him."

"A rifle?"

"No, his revolver. He used it, because where he used to wait was just a short distance from the road," she said.

"And so when he went on these hunts for Mr. Keys and laid in waiting, did this occur a number of times?"

"Yes, several times. I couldn't tell you how many times he used to be over there waiting for him to come along. And

166

where the shooting finally did take place was where he used to be so many times—right near where the sign was posted."

"Now during Mr. Keys' trial, the prosecuting attorney presented two claims which conflicted about Mr. Bagley. One was that he was running away when he was shot by Mr. Keys. The other one was that he was crouched on the ground. What would you say, as to the claim that Mr. Bagley was running away?"

"Well, Mr. Kilpatrick, I would say no, that he wasn't running away. He often told me that he wished he could meet Mr. Keys alone. Worth said that Mr. Keys thought himself such a crack shot, but Worth thought that he could beat Mr. Keys to what he called 'the draw' any time. I'm almost certain that he wasn't running away."

"Then you think that it wasn't in Worth Bagley's makeup to run away?"

"No, it wasn't," she answered. "He just thought he could beat Mr. Keys to the draw. He wasn't a coward, and he wasn't afraid. But I'm almost sure, as I was out there, that Mr. Keys shot only in self-defense. I know that Worth took the first shot at him."

Then the State Assemblyman turned to a different subject. "Now, in the course of time that you were out there, did you see Mr. Bagley post any signs on the property that would be a warning to Mr. Keys to stay off?"

"Well, he had signs up all over the property. Right by the house, he had a sign which said, 'Beware of Gun Traps.' I never saw a gun trap there, but he had those signs up which scared all of my friends away."

"Do you think that he put those signs up especially as a warning to Mr. Keys?"

"Yes."

"Did he ever make any remarks as to why he put those signs up?"

"Oh, yes. He said he felt he would be within the law in case Mr. Keys came within the property, and he shot him."

"And that he wouldn't be liable for murder?" he asked.

"That's right. He often talked of making a shooting range out of part of our place—where Mr. Keys used to cross over

167

to go east to his mine. He even spoke of this to the San Bernardino County Deputy."

"Which deputy was that?"

"Mr. Stocker, who's now Sheriff. He said he would make a shooting range of this place. He also said that if Mr. Keys went by, and he shot him, that it would be Mr. Keys' own fault for going across the shooting range."

"Did Mr. Bagley seem to be in league with Mr. Stocker of the Sheriff's office?"

"Yes, of San Bernardino."

"What instances took place to make you think that they were acting together?" he asked her.

"Well, it was this fence that Mr. Keys put up. His cattle had been running, and Mr. Bagley had spoken to him about it. So Mr. Keys asked for permission to put up a fence."

"Who is Mr. Lawrence?"

"He was out there at the time and was running a few head of cattle which he brought out from Oceanside where he lives."

"And Mr. Keys and Mr. Lawrence had a mutual interest in wanting to put up their fence so their stock could graze?"

"Yes, that's right," she answered immediately. "Mr. Bagley used to watch them with his rifle from a distance. He often said if they ever went near the well that he would shoot them, and the fence that they were building went down by the well. Why, they hadn't even completed the fence when they were ordered off the place."

"And that was while you were there?" he asked.

"Yes. He ordered them off of the place while I was there. You have a picture of the fence, I think," she said, pointing to the small stack of photographs that rested on the coffee table in front of Kilpatrick. "I believe that the picture there shows the cow catcher or whatever it is—the guard."

"The cattle guard."

"Yes. Well, that's as far as they got with the fence. They got in the cattle guard there," she said, picking up the photograph, "and then you can see the sign that Worth put up." She handed the photograph to him. "He told them they couldn't use it, and that they would have to keep off of the property."

"Then Mr. Keys couldn't use the property even after he put up the fence?"

"Yes, that was all a waste on Mr. Keys' part. At the time Mr. Stocker was out there, he knew of the affair. I think he should have done something about it—of course, it was just a verbal agreement with Mr. Keys."

"Did Mr. Keys ever molest Mr. Bagley or you in any way?"

"No, in no way at all, but Worth went out of his way to antagonize Mr. Keys."

"Now, Miss Clark, tell me about Mr. Keys as a neighbor and about his development of the community," the Assemblyman asked.

"Well, Mr. Keys was the only man out there—I am of course speaking about the time I was out there—who made a living off of his land and who improved it. He had cows and chickens, and he raised a garden and fruit trees. In fact, he raised a garden large enough so that he was able to sell vegetables to the little store in Yucca Valley. He made a living off of his land, and he was the only one out there that ever did. The other people at that time were living on the county or they had small pensions."

"Did Mr. Keys develop any roads?"

"Well, he developed all of the roads out there, and he built a schoolhouse on his property. The nearest other facility was twenty-five miles away, so he worked hard to get a school established there for his children. He built a cabin for its teachers, supplied them with water, and kept up the school. He took care of it all."

"And Mr. Keys was the only one out there who had tried to improve his land. He had tried to preserve the natural beauty, which is more than outsiders have done. Worth did everything against the law out there. He chopped down the Christmas trees that I told you about. He had quail traps which were very much against the law, and there were Indian relic caves out there that he destroyed. There was one

169

cave that he just boarded and used as a place to store dynamite. At another place, my brother and I found hieroglyphics all over the top. Well, Worth destroyed them. So where Mr. Keys tried to preserve the beauty of the area, Worth just didn't have any regard for it at all."

"While we are on the subject," she said, "Mr. Keys always tried to cooperate with everybody up in that country. For instance, if anyone would make a complaint about his cattle crossing on their property, Mr. Keys would put up a fence. The others would just go through the property and leave the gates open. Worth did that several times on purpose. And speaking of fences, there was another incident relating to them. Mr. Keys had asked Worth if he could put up this little fence that was just a short one to keep his cattle from Worth's property. Mr. Keys put up the fence, and a week later Worth cut it into shreds. I was out there at the time," she said definitely.

"Can you say anything about Mr. Bagley's resources? How did he make a living?" Kilpatrick asked her.

"Well, he had his Sheriff's pension from Los Angeles County. I was informed from the office down there that the only reason that they gave him the pension was to get rid of him, because he wasn't liked. I went down to see Mr. Schaefer at the Investigative Department of the Sheriff's Office. He told me that he had worked with Worth for some time, and that he finally asked to be transferred because he couldn't stand the cruelty that Worth inflicted on the prisoners at the Los Angeles County jail, especially when they were going up in the elevator."

"You gave us the name of a man at Mac's Radio Shop in Twentynine Palms. What was his connection?"

"Well, I gave you that because he had heard Worth say that he was going to shoot Mr. Keys, if he ever caught him alone. I don't know if he will testify to that or not. There are so many people out there who are afraid to say anything because of the business that they are in, and they are more or less under the protection of the Sheriff of San Bernardino County," she said.

"There's a road that Mr. Keys used which was on Mr.

Bagley's property. What do you remember about Mr. Keys using it?"

"Yes, he used to go across the property. When he went across, Worth would sometimes shoot with his high-powered rifle. The marks are still on the rocks out there."

"And what was the reason for his shooting across the road?"

"Well, he said some time Mr. Keys might be going across there. If he were just target shooting and Mr. Keys got in the way, there was nothing that he could do about it. So you see he liked to antagonize Mr. Keys. Oh, I remember something else. Mr. Keys had two very nice daughters, and Worth often said that he would like to catch one of them alone sometime," she concluded.

Mr. Kilpatrick sat there a moment taking in everything that Isabelle Clark had stated for the deposition that his assistant was in the process of transcribing. He could see that this lady was not well. Her eyes looked tired, and the paleness of her skin indicated to him that she didn't get outside very often. He was thankful that she had consented to this talk, and wanted to minimize the strain of discussing her ill-fated marriage to Worth Bagley.

"Just a few more questions if you please. Do you want to say anything about the state of your health as a result of your association with Worth Bagley?"

"Oh definitely," she replied. "Before I met him I was getting along wonderfully. The desert had done me worlds of good. But after that time—that is, after living with him that short time—I have been going downhill ever since."

Then Kilpatrick had one more subject to discuss. "Did the big cattlemen try to run Mr. Keys out?"

"Yes, that's right. Mr. Keys was the first settler up there. He tried to improve his property in every way. He just wanted to make a living for his little family and to be left strictly alone. Well, that didn't happen, because people came up there just to make trouble for him."

"Did he seem to get along all right with this Mr. Lawrence who you say came in and helped him build a fence?" Kilpatrick inquired.

171

"Yes, he got along with Mr. Lawrence until the San Bernardino officials got a hold of Mr. Lawrence and talked to him. After that there was always trouble. Finally, Lawrence left the country."

"Did it appear to you that the San Berardino officials were in with the big cattlemen aiding Mr. Bagley and causing trouble for Mr. Keys?"

"Yes, that's right. The San Bernardino officials had cattle up there, but it seems to me that all of these people were just jealous of Mr. Keys. He was the first settler out there. Naturally he had the best property there—the property with the lake on it, and the wells. They were jealous of him, and he improved the place," she concluded.

"I believe that is all the questions that I have. You have been most helpful. Thank you."

While the typing of her deposition was being completed, Isabelle talked quietly with her guest. Kilpatrick could see that she was tiring. Her appearance was mute testimony to her long bout with tuberculosis. Little did either of them realize that day how seriously ill she was—with an illness which would cause her premature death within two years.

The typing was now finished. After Isabelle had read her transcribed statement, she signed her name, then handed it to the State Assemblyman. It would be instrumental in helping to bring justice to Bill Keys.

XXIII

October 27, 1948
Wednesday

For several weeks the date had been circled on the calendar that hung in the kitchen of the Desert Queen Ranch. As Frances sat there at the large oak table each evening enjoying the late meal that she shared with Phyllis, her blue eyes would frequently wander to the circled date on the opposite wall. October 25th. How long she had hoped and waited for that day to come. Each time that she looked at the date she knew exactly how many days were left until Bill would be coming home to the family, ranch, and desert that he loved.

Later after they had cleared the table, she stood at the sink washing their dishes. As Frances stared through the window into the outside darkenss, she saw her face reflected in the glass and realized there had been a lot of changes here in the five and a half years of Bill's absence. Her hair was now completeley white, and she felt much older. Like the scrub oak that grew outside just a few feet in front of her, her children had grown into adults. Two of them were married. Even though she and Phyllis had kept busy around the place, she thought about all of the work that still needed to be done—work that was too heavy or too involved for either of them to do—but she took solace in the thought that Bill would soon be back and then everything would once again return to normal.

She knew from his letters that Erle Stanley Gardner had been busy in the three months since Isabelle had given her deposition. He and Vernon Kilpatrick had worked long hours assembling the evidence that they had collected in Bill's behalf. When they were certain they had enough proof, they acted. They asked the California Adult Authority for a hearing.

The five member board of the Adult Authority met periodically to consider the prison records of sentenced persons to determine when they might be released. As the governor's advisory board, they also had the authority to parole individuals, as well as to pass on recommendations for pardons. Normally because of the number of cases that must be considered at each of their sessions, little time could be devoted to individual cases. But because of Gardner's special request, as well as Kilpatrick's position as a State Assemblyman, the board agreed to meet at a special session and to give them an entire day if necessary.

Gardner sat with them in the morning and in machine-gun fashion presented the facts of the case, Dr. Snyder's findings, his own, the reports of Bagley's doctors, and proved that errors had been presented during Bill's trial. That afternoon Kilpatrick had his turn with the board. He presented Isabelle Clark's deposition, as well as her previous statement made at the time of her divorce from Bagley. By the end of the sessions the board members were convinced that Bill Keys had been wrongly convicted.

Even a review of Bill's prison record indicated to them that he was a model prisoner and would gain nothing by remaining there any longer. But a pardon takes time to execute, so it was once again recommended that Bill be released on parole until the time that he could be granted a full pardon by the Governor. Later that same day, Gardner met with Bill and told him of their decision. He requested that his friend accept their offer of parole. Bill agreed, and Monday, October 25th was the date set for his release from San Quentin.

Frances was already on her way to San Francisco over the weekend being driven by her friends, Mr. and Mrs. John Webb. They met Bill as he walked out the front gates on Monday morning and on the following day started the long return trip home.

On Wednesday afternoon at 4:30 the Webbs' car arrived in Joshua Tree at the Shell gas station owned by Pat and her husband, Bob Garry. Phyllis was there along with several close family friends who greeted Bill warmly. Then the group formed a car caravan and headed up into the Monument to the ranch.

As the procession pulled into the front yard, other family members and friends poured out of the house to greet their arrival. Bill was happy to see Virginia and her husband, Ray, who had come down from San Francisco for the occasion. Chet and Lee Perkins, old friends for many years, were there too. Even Willis was there. He had been released from the army several months earlier and had decided to return to the desert to try his luck at mining. With three of his former service buddies, they started working the Desert Queen Mine and were living in the cabin at the Wall Street Mill. Willis introduced his friends to his father, who was surprised to see so many people turn out for his homecoming.

It wasn't long until the entire group moved into the wood frame house to talk and to enjoy the dinner that his daughters had prepared for them. It was a day that most of them would never forget, especially Bill and Frances. For as they walked together across the front yard, they both knew that Bill had his long awaited freedom, and he was home to stay.

XXIV

August 1, 1956
Wednesday

Although nearly seventy-seven years old, he still walked and worked with the ease of a much younger man. Gone was his Van Dyke beard of much earlier days, but when friends drew closer to the deeply tanned man, they could see that Bill Keys had changed very little in the eight years since his return from prison.

This August afternoon found him out amongst the pear trees of his once larger orchard, as he inspected the fruit on each. "Only a couple more weeks," he thought to himself. "Then they'll be ready." He knew that Frances was already anticipating her last canning activities for the summer. She had saved some of her remaining jars and lids for the pears, after her other vegetables and fruits had been processed and put safely away for winter's use.

Completing his inspection, Bill walked several yards from the trees toward the side of the house to locate the valve in the main irrigation pipe that crossed above the orchard area. When he turned its handle, water poured out, falling into the channel that he had previously cut to direct its flow down toward the trees. There the channel branched allowing the water to pool around the base of each tree and then to be slowly absorbed into the ground.

He stood there watching the flow, realizing that without a steady supply of water, his life on the desert would have been quite different. He would have had no orchard, garden, or mill to process his gold ore. His gaze shifted upwards to his water's source high in the rocks across the wash. There was his lake, held in check by a concrete dam. Since his return, he had raised its walls even higher to make it deeper. This ultimately required him to construct two more dams further up the wash to hold the lake's increased capacity, as it began to overflow through the rocks in these areas.

These construction projects had been a monumental undertaking requiring long hours, hard work, and ingenuity. The sheer cost of materials would have been a stumbling block to most area residents, but Bill traded for the cement and relied on his own stockpile of materials already at the ranch. Almost singlehandedly, he had built the forms for the walls out of scrap lumber and driven the steel rods into the granite boulders to firmly anchor the sides of the dam. From the rocks above he anchored heavy cables. Across them rode the steel bucket carrying the heavy load of concrete from the mixer to the section being poured.

As the walls grew higher, Bill increased the height of the scaffolding in front of it. Across it he moved as agilely as the desert bighorn sheep who frequently drank from his lake. Back and forth he moved, mixing and then pouring. Into the wet concrete he placed scrap steel and rocks for additional support. Later when the dam was complete, even professional engineers marveled at its solid construction and Bill's self-taught engineering ability.

After a doctor friend from Vallejo traded him a new jeep for his Gold Tiger Mine, he used it for transportation and for dragging additional rock boulders to his ranch. Using a sledge hammer and chisel, he cut holes deep in the granite slabs, then drove in wooden wedges. These were soaked with water. When the wood expanded, the rock broke exactly where Bill had planned. Some of these rock blocks were stacked out in the wash to build a new garden wall. Behind it he placed discarded cans, bottles and trash, covering them with sand and sediments dredged from the lake. When it was completed, the additional space added a quarter more land to his orchard and garden area.

These and a multitude of other jobs kept Bill busy at the

ranch, but he still found time to prospect, to build another dam at Cow Camp, and to raise the walls of the existing Barker Dam. Even Frances, Virginia, and Phyllis helped him with that one, and their names were set into the wet concrete at the top of the wall at its completion in 1949, bearing silent testimony to their accomplishment.

Bill's attention was directed from his watering chores when he noticed a cloud of dust moving in the distance along the road which dead-ended at their house.

"Mother, we've got company," he called, as he walked by the side of the house out into its front yard. In a few minutes he saw the blue-green Ford sedan, as it crossed the wash and came over the small rise into the front yard and stopped. The vehicle was familiar at the ranch, as were its occupants.

"It's Gwyn and Willie," he called again, as Frances came out of the kitchen door to join him. They were always happy to see their only living son, who had only been married since the previous January. They had warmly welcomed his attractive wife into their family, and both were happy that the couple had decided to live in nearby Joshua Tree in the house that Willie had built for Gwyn several years earlier.

"Dad, we have your mail plus this one from the Governor's office!" Gwyn said excitedly as she got out of the car and handed Bill a sealed cardboard tube.

"Here, Mother," Bill said, handing the official looking tube to Frances.

The four walked over near the house to sit in the chairs under the large Pinyon pine. Frances' trembling hands worked at the unyielding wrappings, but with Willie's assistance she finally opened the tube and extracted two papers rolled inside. Unrolling the first one, she saw that it was a typewritten letter from Goodwin J. Knight, the Governor of California. Adjusting her glasses, she read the letter to her waiting family:

July 26, 1956

Mr. William F. Keys
Keys Ranch
P.O. Box 114
Joshua Tree, California

178

Dear Mr. Keys:

I have considered your application for a pardon following completion of your sentence in a California State Prison.

I noted from this application and the supporting evidence that you have lived an honest and upright life since your discharge from custody, conducted yourself with sobriety and industry, exhibited good moral character, and conformed to and obeyed the laws of the land.

It is a great personal satisfaction to me to recognize that you have in this way earned the right of favorable consideration and have demonstrated yourself worthy of a full and unconditional pardon.

Accordingly, I have granted you a pardon and I am enclosing a copy.

> Sincerely,
> Goodwin J. Knight
> Governor

Then Frances unrolled the second piece of paper and read its contents:

PARDON

There has been submitted to this office an application for pardon on behalf of William F. Keys, also known as William F. Keys, San Quentin No. 71407, who was convicted of manslaughter in Riverside County during August 1943, and received a sentence of 0 to 10 years. He served 4 years and 7 months in prison and 1 year, 4 months on parole, being discharged therefrom on February 28, 1950.

On July 12, 1956, the Adult Authority made the following recommendation:

On that date the Adult Authority recommended that subject's application for pardon be granted. The Adult Authority believes this recommendation to be justified in view of applicant's adjustment during the past eight years, his age, and the added fact that he has a worthy motive in desiring to again vote as a citizen and to re-establish his family's name in society. Applicant has constantly maintained that he shot his victim in self-defense. Since his release on parole, he has evidenced satisfactory conduct. It is pointed out that this case was highly publicized some years ago and was investigated by an Assembly Interim Committee during 1948.

Through the years Keys had maintained his innocence. His present plea was based on this claim. However, the records fail to fully substantiate clemency upon this ground. The Adult Authority does feel that his social adjustment is such to make him worthy of clemency upon the grounds of rehabilitation.

NOW THEREFORE, in view of the foregoing favorable recommendation, I, GOODWIN J. KNIGHT, Governor of the State of California, pursuant to the authority vested in me by the Constitution and statutes of the State of California, do hereby grant to William F. Keys, also known as William F. Keys, San Quentin No. 71407, a full and unconditional pardon for the offense hereinbefore referred to.

IN WITNESS WHEREOF, I have hereinto set my hand and caused the Great Seal of California to be affixed this 24th day of July A.D. Nineteen Hundred and Fifty-six.

                (signed) Goodwin J. Knight
                Governor of California
GREAT SEAL

There were tears in her eyes as Frances handed the papers to Bill and said, "There it is, Dad."

They had both waited for this day for so long that neither of them could speak. But no words were necessary to convey the feelings that silently passed between two people who had spent so many years together. Their love and concern for each other was still as strong and would last as long as the granite rocks that looked down upon them.

XXV

The Last Years
1956-1969

The last remaining years at the Desert Queen Ranch were quiet ones for Bill and Frances except when the shouts of visiting grandchildren echoed from canyon rocks. Bill continued his mining interests, spending time in the Pallen Mountains to the east working his gypsum claims. Frances was busy with her own interests and was frequently seen in Joshua Tree at her daughter, Pat's, or visiting there with Evelyn Hutchinson or her other close friends. She still collected purple glass and had one of the best collections in the area. But her main interest was planning the new house that Bill had promised to build for her. This one of brick would be cooler in summer and less drafty in winter than their present house, which was beginning to show its age. This last dream never materialized, as she grew ill and passed away quietly on January 9, 1963 in a Banning hospital. She was seventy-five.

Four days later the Wiefels and Son Chapel in Twenty-nine Palms was filled beyond capacity at her afternoon service. Many persons had waited patiently outside in the near freezing temperatures to bid a last farewell to this gentle pioneer spirit whom they knew as a friend. After the services, she was taken to the local cemetery for burial.

Bill missed Frances beyond words and wanted her to rest forever in the desert canyon that she had loved so much and where she had lived so long. Five months later, after permission was secured from county officials, she came home to rest beside her three sons in the family cemetery at their Desert Queen Ranch.

Bill continued to live at the ranch, caring for it until financial problems resulting from his long legal battles and mounting state taxes forced him to sell it. As part of the sales agreement, Bill was to be allowed to live at the ranch and at his death to be buried there. The new owner was a man from Los Angeles who hoped to develop it into a resort. When these plans proved impossible, he traded it for government land elsewhere, and the ranch became part of Joshua Tree National Monument.

Bill's last five years were almost as active as his previous ones. Although arthritis sometimes slowed him down, he kept busy with his gypsum claims or with projects around the ranch. In May 1966 he was selected as Supreme Marshal of the annual Turtle Days celebration in Joshua Tree. He brought a small stamp mill, crusher, engine and other mining equipment down from the ranch with the help of his long-time friend, Oran Booth. His demonstrations on mining captivated the interest of his audience.

Later that summer he decided to reactivate his Wall Street Mill. A carpenter friend helped him to enclose its machinery, while others helped him put it back into operation for several weeks, after which it was shut down forever.

Bill delighted his frequent ranch visitors with stories about his early adventures with Death Valley Scotty, the era of the cattleman, miner, and homesteader, and of his gunfight with Worth Bagley. Frequently he showed his listeners the gold nuggets he usually carried in his pocket.

Even Park Service rangers were welcome to talk with him. He had softened his earlier animosity when he discovered that they were as concerned as he was about protecting the fragile desert environment. They knew that he had admonished Monument visitors whom he had found picking wildflowers, and they enjoyed his company when he went with them throughout the vast area, pointing out places, cattle tanks, Indian campsites, and old landmarks that few of them knew existed.

One landmark most of them already knew about—a

stone that Bill had carved, hauled with his jeep, and set up on the exact spot that had changed the course of his life. For generations to come, those who walk past this spot will remember what had taken place, as they read Bill's carefully carved letters:

Here is where Worth Bagley
bit the dust at the hand
of W. F. Keys - May 11, 1943

Bill Keys passed away on June 28, 1969. So much interest had been generated in this man of the desert that the local radio station in Joshua Tree, KJST, carried his funeral service live throughout the area. Through the assistance of the telephone company, a temporary line was laid across country from the nearest pole to the ranch to carry the remote broadcast to the station. Other friends and neighbors gathered with the family at the cemetery at the Desert Queen Ranch, as Bill was laid to rest beside Frances. He had come home for the last time to become part of the canyon that he loved and labored for during his sixty years of residence.

*   *   *   *   *

The ranch lies silent now except when coyotes howl from the rock ledges above. Gambel's quail strut where chickens once flocked, sharing their dominion with rabbits and lizards. Restless winds blow through wall chinks and rattle sheets of tin on roof tops. Buildings lean at drunken angles, while neglected machinery rusts with the change of seasons. The trees still survive, although the cracked irrigation pipes no longer carry water from the lake. Packrats and mice stockpiling food and nesting material in the old cars and in the ranch house prove that the homesteading spirit is still very much alive. Seasonal ranger tours give Monument visitors a glimpse of a time period that is no more.

Frequently the ranch tours conclude at the family cemetery. Although Bill had spent considerable time in carving and inlaying granite monuments for Frances and their sons, he had not done one for himself. Rangers who had known him selected a stone from those that he had stored near his Wall Street Mill. For several years it stood blank, marking Bill's resting place until Easter 1978.

Then Willis and Gwyn once more returned to the desert for a visit from their home in the mountain country near Yosemite. Their mission on this trip was to carve Bill's stone and inlay it with the blue copper rock that he had mined earlier. This labor of love required another trip to complete and the resulting artistry would have pleased Bill very much. Hopefully Bill's sentiments had changed from the thoughts that he expressed in a poem sent to friends four years before his death.

"Cruel fate has been my master
To his mandates I must bow
He has ruled me through life's journey,
I care not where he leads me now.

Let the place where I am buried
Be a drear and lonely place,
Let the sunlight shine there dimly,
Let no cheer its loneness grace.

Let my name be never spoken,
And none of me sigh or weep,
May no mound or sign or token,
Mark the place of my last sleep.

Let the night birds sing my dirges,
And the wind my mourners be,
Let the tears be pearly dewdrops,
None but nature weep for me."

Bill's wishes have certainly not materialized. The stories and legends surrounding him are too firmly planted in the desert soil to be blown away by the passage of time. As a result, his name will be remembered by generations to come. Bill would probably be amazed and embarrassed by all of the fuss.

184